INTRODUCTION TO CONTAINER GARDENING

BEGINNERS GUIDE TO GROWING YOUR OWN FRUIT, VEGETABLES AND HERBS USING CONTAINERS AND GROW BAGS

MADISON PIERCE

CONTENTS

COPYRIGHT

Legal Notice:

Disclaimer Notice:

INTRODUCTION

What if I told you that having a thriving crop of all your favorite greens was far easier than you thought? What if reaping the rewards and joys of a beautiful veggie and herb garden didn't mean sunburn, sore knees, and the need for lots of space?

Enter the spotlight; container gardening!

Are you not convinced? Well, it's true. As an avid gardener, I have tried and tested nearly every type of gardening style there is, and I can quite honestly tell you that container gardening is one of my favorites. Not just because it's a space-saving and affordable gardening format, but also because I get to eat my own fresh veggies straight from the garden. When it comes to living holistically, nothing beats "growing your own."

Gardening is certainly not a new kid on the block. It's been around for centuries. First, it was a necessity, a source of livelihood for everyday people like you and me. Families would grow their own crops – it was the norm.

But then urbanization came along, and farming became a business, too. What was once a necessity for every household became obsolete. People could get their fresh produce ready to eat and on-demand at the local grocery store, so gardening entered a new phase. It became *something else* – a source of enjoyment, or a hobby if you will!

Nowadays, home gardeners are in it for the fresh produce, the stress relief it brings, the bonding opportunities it provides, and that sense of achievement that only a perfectly ripened tomato or a gleaming dark green bunch of spinach can provide. The sheer sense of pride and joy in being able to say "I grew that" or "fresh from *our* garden" is unmatched – trust me on that!

If you're new to the idea of gardening or have only held a trowel in your hands on a few and far between occasions, this book is for you, the newbie trying to determine if they're part of the green thumb tribe. This book is for the gardener wanting to have all the joys of gardening, even without a lot of space. This also is for the green thumb at heart, willing and ready to embrace urban gardening!

Container gardening does not discriminate. It's ideal for people with large gardens who don't have the time to tend to an expansive veggie garden. It's just as ideal for people living in city apartments with nothing but a small balcony to use as garden space.

Once you learn the tips, tricks, and techniques of container gardening, you will realize that you can do it successfully just about anywhere.

By now, you're probably wondering who I am and what makes me an authority on the topic of container gardening!

My name is Madison Pierce, and I am not your average city-dweller. When I moved to a big city many years ago, I wanted nothing more than to continue my gardening efforts, but the problem was that I had moved into an apartment with nothing more than a small sunny balcony outside. I immediately set to work investigating various gardening methods that work in small spaces and container gardening stuck. Five years later, and there's no looking back!

I'm not just a regular gardener. I have a passion for it. It's in my blood – or so it seems. And it has become my mission to help as many beginners toying with the idea of gardening to don their gloves, grab some tools and get to work. After all, you will only know if it's a hobby for you and if you can succeed if you start. And isn't today the perfect day to start?

In this guide, you will learn a lot of things about container gardening. When I started writing this book, I intended it to be a full-on guide for beginner gardeners, and that's precisely what it is.

The pages that follow feature helpful information on how to maximize your small space, how to choose veggies and herbs carefully, and what tips and tricks you can use to help your container plants thrive. Your balcony or small space will be the envy of your neighbors, and your fresh produce will pack your home-cooked meals with color and goodness.

I will carefully guide you through everything you need to know based on the trials and tribulations that I faced when I first started. This comprehensive guide is beginner-friendly and ready to help you jumpstart the garden of your dreams!

Without much further ado, let's get started on Chapter One, which focuses on *Preparing for Container Gardening*.

1

PREPARING FOR CONTAINER GARDENING

There's been a misconception for quite some time that gardening is a hobby for people with extensive rolling gardens or lots of outdoor space. Container and grow bag gardening has put this misconception to rest, especially in *my* life.

As a mum and avid gardener, I cannot tell you how rewarding it is to nip into the garden to grab some lettuce, tomatoes, and herbs for a lunchtime salad or spinach and kale for a nutritious supper. It wasn't always like this. For the majority of my life, I bought into the whole hype of buying fresh produce from the grocery store, but now that I've tried my hand at container gardening, there's no looking back. I have discovered a method of gardening that's sustainable and doesn't require much space!

Container and grow bag gardening has become increasingly popular because it's flexible. It is the best solution for those limited to a balcony, a small sunny space in the kitchen, or a tiny yard outback. Gone are the days where all you thought of growing was a few pretty flowers. Now you can grow nutritious fresh fruits and veggies, which will all be within arms reach and without the grocery store price tag attached.

For me, the benefits of container and grow bag gardening are as follows:

- My family enjoys a more diverse and healthy diet
- I save money
- I grow the specific herbs and veggies that we love to eat and no more "making do" with what the grocery store has.
- As a family, we reduce our carbon footprint.
- I get to bond with my family when they lend a helping hand
- I enjoy a sense of achievement which is great for self-care, by the way

Container and grow bag gardening gives an instant splash of color, creates a focal point in the garden, and brings joy to your home. Strawberry baskets or pots can be hung from your porch or placed on a pedestal, a windowsill, or on the ground. If you place containers and grow bags on a deck or patio, you'll add color and ambiance to that outdoor sitting area. You can fill pot clusters with your favorite leafy greens, tomatoes, or culinary herbs. If you get creative about where you place your containers, you may find that you don't need an actual garden at all to enjoy the rewards of container gardening!

This chapter is dedicated to getting you prepared for container gardening by ensuring you've got all the fundamentals covered before digging deeper into the learning process.

HAVING THE RIGHT MINDSET & APPROACH TO GARDENING

For me, container and grow bag gardening is as much fun as it is functional. I have noticed that newbie gardeners give up too soon or don't put in enough effort because things don't go as expected immediately. It takes time and effort, and there will be highs and lows along the way.

The first batch of fresh ripe tomatoes you pick or the first taste of fresh peppery rocket on your homemade salad or pizza will fill you with pride and joy.

Much the same, the first time a grasshopper eats your spinach crop, or you discover your beautiful tomato vines plagued with dreaded red spider mite, there will be tears even if you're only crying on the inside.

As I said, prepare for the highs and lows, each is a learning process.

Document your progress as much as possible. It's exciting to look back on pictures of empty pots and a few months later have pictures of thriving crops to show off.

Before we jump into preparing for container and grow bag gardening, I would like to share one last meaningful tip: make sure that gardening is something you *want* to do. Schedule time each day to check on your plants, do a bit of watering and check that everything is progressing as planned.

If you have this approach to your container and grow bag gardening project, you can expect to excel in the art (yes, it's an art, not just a hobby)!

Below are a few tips and things you need to consider when preparing for container and grow bag gardening.

PROVIDING THE RIGHT LIGHT AND TEMPERATURE

For your container or grow bag garden to thrive, you have to ensure that you provide your veggies and herbs with the correct light and temperature.

Among the many benefits of container and grow bag gardening is that you can still grow splendid plants and vegetables no matter how little direct sunlight your yard receives. It would be best if you chose which veggies and herbs you will grow carefully.

- **Determine how much sun your garden space gets**

Before you pick the plants you want to grow, you need to know how much sunlight your available space gets. Most vegetables and herbs like lots of sunshine, so you will need an area that gets at least 6 hours of direct sunlight. Of course, how much or little sun your space gets will determine how much and how often you water your veggies and herbs.

When you're preparing to get started, choose a sunny day to monitor your space. You can do this by routinely checking how much sunlight it receives every 30 minutes, or you can use a sun calculator. Also, be mindful of the time of the year you'll be planting because the sun's angle will also impact how much sun your available space gets. For example, the sun's angle is different during the winter than in the summer.

A plant's ability to thrive in full sun, dappled sun, or shade depends on how many hours of sunlight it receives daily and, of course, what type of plant it is. For instance, chives and mint are two herbs that thrive in shady spots, but rosemary, lavender, and basil demand full sunshine.

• Position your containers with care

When it comes to ensuring the correct temperature, there are a few things to consider. It's important to note that container plants will heat up and cool off quicker than plants growing in the ground. Your container or grow bag vegetable garden's temperature is influenced by where you choose to place your containers.

South-facing decks or balconies tend to be hotter than those facing north. The material and color of the deck are important, too, as darker colors absorb heat. Ceramic tiles and stucco walls, which absorb and radiate heat, will heat up faster than wood – if you position your containers on these surfaces, you may need to move them around during the hottest seasons of the year.

• Select pots and containers wisely

In addition to your containers' position, the container size and material will also impact plant temperature together with weather conditions. It's not a good idea to use metal or dark-colored containers because they can become very hot and cook the roots. Grouping pots also helps to shield plants from the sun and wind. Using a light-colored mulch inside the pots will keep the soil surface cooler and, in addition, hold moisture.

• Consider soil temperatures

Keep in mind that many plants need soil at a minimum temperature of 60 degrees F (15 C) to survive. You can buy a handy thermometer at your local garden center to check the soil's temperature and ensure your plants' health.

- **Keep outside container plants warm at night**

If you can't move your plants indoors and need to keep them warm at night if the temperature drops, you can cover them with plastic or lightweight blanketing. Another tip is to fill buckets with warm water and place them around your plants during the coldest times to help bring a little warmth and humidity to them. Doing this will ensure heat radiates around your plants during the night, and there's less chance of them falling victim to cold weather and freezing.

I found that every plant needs a certain amount of sunlight, and if you're aiming for thriving crops, you need to provide enough of it. If you buy seeds or seedlings at a garden center, you will probably notice a label that says "full sun", "part sun", or similar. What does it mean? How *much* sun is full sun? Here's a helpful chart to use.

Amount of direct sunlight required	Total hours
Full sun plants	6 – 8 hours
Full sun vegetables	10 hours or more
Part sun/part shade plants	4 – 6 hours
Full shade plants	3 hours

WATERING YOUR CONTAINER OR GROW BAG GARDEN

Giving your plants enough water has to be your priority when container and grow bag gardening. Your plants don't have access to underground moisture, so they dry out much quicker. You are their sole provider of water, and while that can be a powerful feeling, it's also a lot of responsibility. Your container and grow bag veggies and herbs rely on you watering them to stay alive, and if you provide enough water, they will reward you with a bounty of produce!

When watering a container or grow bag plant, it is important to drench the container deeply until water drains from the drainage hole. Ensure you are hydrating the soil thoroughly from top to bottom rather than only on the inside edge or just the surface.

- **Don't over-water**

The amount of water depends on the weather, plant size, and pot size, of course, and it stands to reason that some plants need more water than others. A simple test to see if it is time to water again would be to push your index finger about 1 inch (2.5 cm) into the soil to see if it is drying out.

If the soil is semi-dry, you can water it again. You may notice that your plants follow a pattern. Perhaps your spinach containers seem dry every three days or so, in which case you should set a reminder alarm or calendar event on your mobile phone so that you're always on time with the provision of water.

- **Consider watering tips and hacks – perhaps some will work for you**

Container and grow bag gardening is more high maintenance in summer than it is in winter. On hot days, you will need to give your container plants a thorough watering in the early morning and evening if required, ensuring that you allow the water to soak down to the roots. Plants need ample airflow and moisture to stay cool and moist during the hot summer, so be sure to space each pot appropriately (we will dig a little deeper into this later in the book).

Double Potting Method

One watering hack is to use the double-potting method. Double-potting is an easy way to ensure your plants' health and is done by placing a small container inside a larger one filled with sphagnum moss or crumpled newspapers. Water the plant and the filler in between the pots at the same time. This method provides better water retention, stabilizes the temperature, and protects the plant from the wind.

Self-Watering Pots

Self-watering containers are excellent for people who cannot water pots every day or travel regularly. Self-watering pots have a reservoir section that holds water to keep the soil in the container moist. You don't have to buy anything expensive if you want a self-watering container. In fact, with self-watering spikes that you can fill up and push them into the container soil, you can convert any container into a self-watering pot.

USING QUALITY SOIL FOR YOUR PLANTS

The type and quality of soil that you provide to your veggies and herbs will impact whether your plant thrives or not. If you want container vegetables and herbs that produce healthy crops, you need to start with excellent quality soil.

Something to be aware of is that while you can buy "potting soil" at the local garden center, it's not really *soil* – it's a growing medium. It's nothing like the soil in your garden beds, and there's a reason why you should start your pots off with a dedicated potting mix instead of buying topsoil or scooping soil from your garden.

Unfortunately, your garden soil or topsoil may be contaminated with soil-borne pests and weeds. Potting soil formulated explicitly for veggies and herbs is also lightweight and moisture-retentive, a dream-growing environment for vegetables and herbs.

A veggie and herb potting mix or container soil is a sterile growing medium with organic and inorganic components. It lacks living organisms such as parasites, insects, and other minerals typically found in garden soil. Because it is limited to a smaller space, it needs a few extra features to provide balance, sufficient air pockets, water flow, and water retention.

Aside from holding moisture well, the soil needs good drainage to keep the roots healthy. Veggies and herbs can't stand sitting in water for extended periods and may wither or be prone to root rot if your soil traps moisture and doesn't drain well.

I typically prefer potting mixes instead of potting soil, as I experience far more yield from my plants. An excellent potting mix combines peat or coir, pine bark, vermiculite, or perlite. It is interesting to note perlite, vermiculite, and sphagnum moss are often found in potting soil, but I do not recommend using it if they also contain soil. Choose a product that is sterile and has no soil in it. Look for lightweight bags and stay away from products with no ingredients listed.

If you're interested in spending a bit of extra time making things perfect, you could try making your own potting soil by mixing peat moss, perlite, or vermiculite and well-decomposed compost in an equal ratio.

While you don't have to completely change the soil of your potted plants each season, it's a good idea to top them up and churn fresh nutrient-rich soil into the pot's existing soil as this replenishes nutrients that were consumed that season.

FEEDING YOUR PLANTS

Keeping your container plants healthy requires regular feeding. Fertilizing potted plants is as simple as preparing a nutrient solution and pouring it over the soil mix. The roots absorb the fertilizer and quickly replenish the soil with essential nutrients.

However, you will eventually run out of nutrients in your potting mix because potted veggies and herbs use them up quickly, and every time you water containers and grow bags, nutrients leach out. As a result, plants grown in containers and grow bags require more frequent feeding than plants grown in a garden bed.

- **Add nutrients to your potting soil**

Additionally, because most potting soils do not provide your plants with adequate nutrients, you need to add nutrients to the mix so they can flourish. You can use fish emulsion, seaweed extract, or compost tea to fertilize and feed twice a week in the beginning and adjust based on the plant's response.

- **Fertilize/Feed your plants**

You can also add a slow-release fertilizer to the potting mix. You can do this by combining potting soil and fertilizer in a bucket before using a spade or your hands to turn it into the growing medium in your containers and grow bags. Alternatively, you can start with soil in the pot and then add fertilizer as you go.

Foliar feeding is another way of providing your plant with essential nutrients immediately. Foliar feeding involves applying fertilizer through leaf pores, which effectively boosts fast-growing plants like veggies and herbs.

- **Understand what's in your fertilizers**

Before investing in fertilizers, you need to understand what's in them and how they benefit the specific types of plants you are growing.

Fertilizers contain nitrogen, potassium, and phosphorus. These are essential for healthy plant growth and development. Let's break down each ingredient below:

1. Nitrogen: promotes green growth and overall plant health. Fertilizers high in nitrogen are suitable for leafy greens such as lettuce, Swiss chard, Brussels sprouts, cabbage, cauliflower, potato, broccoli, Asian greens, and leeks. Organic sources include blood meal, feather meal, and liquid fish emulsion.
2. Phosphorus: promotes healthy roots and is vital for fruit and flower development. Fertilizers high in phosphorus are good for blooming plants like

tomatoes and peppers. Organic sources include bone meal, seabird guano, and liquid blends.

3. Potassium: promotes stem growth and overall plant vigor. Fertilizers high in potassium are suitable for root crops such as carrots, beets, and potatoes. Organic sources include Sul-Po-mag, palm bunch ash, and liquid fertilizers.

While compost is a great way to feed your plants, the nutrients will inevitably drain from the soil as the plants grow and bloom. To achieve the best results, add organic fertilizers such as worm castings and fish emulsion during the growing season. You can add more nutrition to your containers by replanting them annually with a fresh mix of compost, garden soil, and coir.

The benefits and instructions of each type of fertilizer may vary, so read the label and follow the instructions carefully. Always follow the guidelines, as over-fertilizing could end up stunting or destroying your crop.

CREATING OPTIMAL DRAINAGE

Last but not least, drainage is crucial in determining if your plants live or die. Many people take drainage for granted and become discouraged from continuing their container and grow bag gardening journey because their plants aren't doing well and don't know why.

One thing you don't want to do is drown your plants. Because of this, your container or grow bag must provide sufficient drainage so that when you water them, the water will pass through the container/bag, and the soil will hold onto some for the plant to make use of as needed. Optimal drainage is happiness for container veggies and herbs.

If your plants sit in soil that is soggy and waterlogged, you're in for a whirlwind of problems such as root rot and fungus infection. Moisture also invites a variety of diseases and insect infestations, so you don't want too much of it hanging out. The solution? Good drainage!

A suitable container or grow bag will have one large hole or several holes in the bottom to allow for drainage. If you find a container or pot that you absolutely love but doesn't have suitable drainage, be prepared to drill, cut, or punch additional holes into the bottom of the pot. You can easily punch holes into a plastic pot with a hammer and pointed tool (awl, large nail, or screwdriver). If you're working with a ceramic or terracotta pot, you can drill holes into it with a masonry drill bit – it's as easy as that. If you are using a grow bag, you can use a pair of scissors to cut a hole, although most plastic grow bags have holes, and the fabric bags are made from materials that naturally drain well.

Keep in mind that the holes should be at least 1/2 inch (1.25 cm) wide for small and medium-sized pots and 1 inch (2.5 cm) wide for large pots. Ensure that no dirt gets trapped in the drainage holes, and ensure that you don't place containers directly onto surfaces that can block the water flow.

Top Tip:

> *Grab a handful of pebbles or gravel and pop them at an odd angle over the drainage holes before filling the pot with soil or growing medium, as this will deter the soil from getting blocked in the drainage hole. It will help if you place the container on either bricks or stones to keep it above the ground to allow the pot to drain more efficiently.*

If your vessel seems to drain too well and your containers and grow bags are drying out quickly, consider using water-absorbing crystals that turn into a gel once wet. This gel traps water and only releases it into the soil when it starts to dry out.

Some people make use of hydromats, which I found aren't entirely necessary. If you want to provide more water retention for your plants, you can line your pots/containers with hydromats, which are water-absorbant. These release water slowly into the soil after you have drenched the container with water. In this way, you can extend the time between watering, which is ideal if you're going on holiday or travel often for work.

Now that you understand the basics and are generally prepared to start container and grow bag gardening, we can turn to the next chapter, which focuses on choosing the proper container, pot, grow bag, or similar for the veggies and herbs you plan to grow.

2

THE RIGHT CONTAINER FOR YOU

When you think about container gardening, you probably think of the plastic pots you can buy at the hardware store, garden center, or nursery. I have news for you! Container and grow bag gardening is not limited to containers and pots.

If you're feeling adventurous, and you probably will be, you can do container gardening in grow bags, plastic bags, trash bags, old tins, and plastic containers. You could get even more creative with other interesting vessels like old appliances or that bath you hauled out when you refurbished the house, a dilapidated wheelbarrow – let your imagination run wild.

That's one of the reasons container gardening is so exciting for me. It's such a creative hobby, and while some rules apply to gardening techniques and know-how, the objects you choose to garden in is really up to you. I always feel good after creating an attractive focal point in the garden or on the balcony that also provides fresh food for us to enjoy. It's like a little piece of *me* goes into each of my container gardening areas.

I would like to introduce you to various vessels that you can use for container gardening. I find each option intriguing, but it's best to pick a pot type that suits your needs and preferences. Be aware, however, of any pitfalls each option has attached to it. Let's jump right in.

WOODEN CONTAINERS

Wooden containers are interesting because you can buy them already made or make them up yourself. If you're fond of DIY woodworking projects or have someone in the family keen to make them up for you, you can piece together aesthetically pleasing wooden planters that fit in with your current décor. Wooden planters look great and add visual value to any space – there's no denying that.

If you're going to buy wooden planters, you need to know the planters will be susceptible to rot as it's a natural product which means they won't last forever. Avoid using raw wood planters outside. I highly recommend that you have the wooden pots treated to withstand long-term exposure to the elements and be somewhat waterproof.

Lining the inside of a wooden planter with plastic is an excellent idea to ensure that water impacts it minimally. Use a thick 6 ml polyethylene sheeting that is used most commonly in greenhouses. You don't have to buy thick plastic, though. You can also use plastic trash bags – make sure you fold them in half to create a double-layer of protection.

You should still cut a hole in the plastic above the drainage hole so that the planter doesn't trap water. Place a small section of mesh screen or permeable landscaping fabric over the drainage hole to ensure the drainage hole doesn't trap soil.

Wooden planters are ideal for growing flowers and vegetables, and they are also good vessels for herbs.

SELF-WATERING CONTAINERS

Self-watering containers are ideal for people who are busy or travel often. They are also great for watering a plant positioned in an awkward spot and for over-zealous waterers. I used to be one of those, but I quickly learned that providing too much water is just as bad as providing too little.

Self-watering containers are great for growing veggies and herbs. They provide consistent moisture directly to the roots of the plants, and by doing so, they improve the plant's health and overall yield.

A decent self-watering container doesn't keep the soil saturated at all times. Instead, it gives your plant just the right amount of water needed to thrive.

You may be wondering how on earth a self-watering container works. They're based on a relatively simple concept, with each self-watering container having a reservoir system – a water storage tank situated at the bottom of the container. You fill the reservoir, so you aren't entirely removed from the equation, and if it becomes too full, it simply drains away through the overflow hole. The soil inside the container soaks water up from the bottom of the container.

Your plants will enjoy consistent water delivered directly to their roots as long as the reservoir tank is full. You don't have to worry about the sun or wind depleting the water too soon as the tank protects the supply from the elements.

One of the benefits I enjoy about self-watering pots is that the leaves of your veggies and herbs are kept dry during the watering process, making them less susceptible to fungus, disease, and insect infestation.

You can buy ready-to-use self-watering containers at most nurseries and garden centers. You can also make your own out of old storage bins, buckets, and other DIY items.

Below are a few steps for making a self-watering container. I have tried this out a few times, and the results are fantastic.

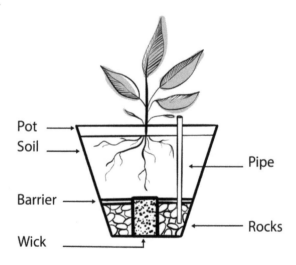

The average self-watering container consists of the following things:

- Container with no holes
- PVC or copper pipe
- A protective layer (window screen, plastic, or old grocery bags)
- Wick (you can use an old plastic bottle)

- Rocks or pebbles
- Soil
- Cat litter box gravel without chemicals (also called Kitty Litter)

Step 1:

- Prepare your wick, which is the plastic bottle.
- Place the bottle into your container and mark it with a marker where the bottle is the ¼ height of the container.
- Cut the bottle where you marked it, and then poke holes into it all along the sides and along the bottom.

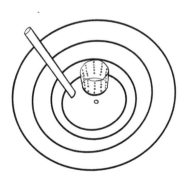

Step 2:

- Ready the pipe and drain hole.
- You can do this by placing the pipe into the container and cutting it down to size.
- It should peep over the container by around 2 inches (5 cm).
- Place the plastic bottle (the wick) into the container and measure where you should drill a drainage hole – this will be right under the top of the wick.
- This is an essential part of the process as it will help avoid root rot.

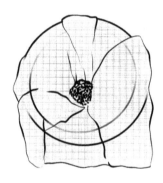

Step 3:

- Fill the wick and place it correctly.
- Do this by positioning the wick in the center of the container.
- Cut a piece of window screen or plastic that is at least two and a half times the diameter of your container. Find the center of the screen and then push it into the plastic bottle (wick).

- Open the screen up to work on the inside - add soil to the bottle on top of the wick.
- Using your hands, pack the soil tightly by pushing it down.

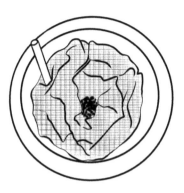

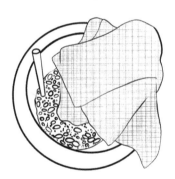

Step 4:

- Insert the rocks and watering pipe.
- First, ensure the wick bottle is in the middle of the container.
- Position the pipe on the side of the container as

depicted in the illustration above and below.
- Position a few rocks to hold the pipe in place.
- Then position rocks around the wick without trapping the window screen/plastic.
- Continue stacking rocks until they reach the same height as the top of the wick bottle.
- Then, push the screen downwards to form a layer over the rocks.
- This will form the protective layer of the pot and ensure the rocks are kept firmly in place.

Step 5:

- Add your soil and plants.
- Do this by carefully spading the soil into the pot.
- Start from the center of the container and work outward toward the sides of the pot.
- Ensure the screen only covers the rocks and not the wick during the process.
- Push the screen down as you're spading the soil in to make sure that it packs firmly. Keep in mind you need to leave sufficient space for your plant.
- Place your plant into the pot and place the remaining soil around the plant.

- Planting depth is important, ensuring that the plant's roots are entirely covered and that the container is full almost right to the top.

Step 6:

- Water your plant and watch it thrive.
- Keep in mind that you have just transplanted your plant, so you need to water the container from the top first.
- It will be the only time you will water your plant on the soil's surface.
- Then, pour water down the pipe until you see water pouring out the drilled drainage hole.
- When watering the plant again, only pour water into the pipe, and the roots will help themselves to what they need directly from the wick.

CERAMIC CONTAINERS

If you're keen to use ceramic containers, I recommend glazed ceramic containers, terracotta pots, and food-grade ceramic containers. Glazed ceramic pots are, of course, waterproof, so they don't suffer the same affliction as unglazed ceramic pots, which often prove challenging to keep moist.

Of course, you don't have to let the difficulty of retaining moisture put you off. You can use plastic lining or hydromats inside the container to retain more water. I find this works well, but you need to be careful of leaving these lined pots outside during the winter.

If temperatures drop below freezing, they can crack or shatter as they retain moisture. If you're dead-set on using ceramic or terracotta pots, take them indoors during the winter.

There are some great benefits of using ceramic pots over and above aesthetics. For starters, they ensure sufficient air to the roots, and because they are typically heavier than other pots, they aren't easily blown over in the wind or bumped over. During the summer months, they will protect the roots of your veggies from absorbing excess heat.

GROW BAGS

Other than plastic containers, grow bags are my next favorite. Grow bags are far more versatile than you might think, and they are available in various materials, shapes, sizes, and depths. They are excellent for growing flowers, veggies, and herbs, and if you can get a big enough size, you can even grow fruit trees in them.

Grow bags are useful in that they make it easy for a plant to self-prune. When the growing roots encounter an air pocket, the plant prunes the root itself and creates a side bud. A great side effect is your plant's roots won't circle the pot, which is often the case with plastic containers. Because of self-pruning, a strong and fibrous root system can develop and ensure the root hairs have a bigger surface for absorbing nutrients.

Popular grow bags include:

- Plastic
- Double layer polypropylene
- Felt
- Non-woven fabrics

I am not a massive fan of plastic grow bags because they can retain heat and cook the roots if the temperatures rise. I like the non-woven, felt, and polypropylene grow bags as they are breathable, which is crucial to the plant's health. They also allow for good drainage, prevent root rot, and provide sufficient nutrients and water to the plant.

One of the things I love about using grow bags is that they don't tear or wear easily when used outdoors. I often find that plastic containers exposed to the sun can become brittle and break, but many of my fruit trees, veggies, and herbs are growing in plastic containers very successfully.

If you opt for using grow bags, choose a product made from fabric (not plastic) that has reinforced seams and stitched corners, as this ensures they last longer. If you buy a decent quality grow bag, you should get several seasons of use out of it.

Keep in mind that grow bags are not ideal for *every* plant. They are particularly useful for plants with a small root system.

Below is a list of veggies, herbs, and fruit that do well in grow bags:

- Tomatoes
- Lettuce
- Radishes
- Pumpkins

- Chilis
- Kale
- Cucumber
- Carrots
- Spinach
- Rocket
- Coriander
- Basil
- Rosemary
- Parsely
- Strawberries
- Oranges (and other citrus)
- Apples
- Blueberries
- Figs
- Plumbs
- Garlic

Nitrogen and other nutrients are added to the grow bag and will last the growing season.

RAISED CONTAINERS

Raised containers, which are also referred to as "raised beds," are structures that enable you to create a protected garden bed above the ground. There are two types of raised containers on the market.

1. Bottomless raised bed: This version is when garden beds are dug directly into the soil and have a frame or structure around them. The soil level is raised above the surface of the ground that surrounds it.
2. Enclosed raised beds: these are either fabric, wood, metal, or plastic with a bottom – sometimes plastic or fabric that helps retain the soil within the structure.

If your soil is unsuitable for planting or if you want to build a garden bed on a hard surface such as a balcony or walkway, raised containers can be convenient.

Using raised garden beds is also suitable if you live in a damp climate and your soil struggles to dry out in between watering. Raised garden beds typically have good drainage, which can assist in avoiding disease, mold, and infestations that can arise from too much moisture.

Raised containers also offer the benefit of the soil warming up quicker (soil in the ground takes far longer to warm up). I must point out, though, that you may need to give your raised containers some added protection during the winter as your plant's roots will be more exposed to the cold.

CONCRETE CONTAINERS

Concrete is a tricky topic when it comes to container gardening. You may not know this, but concrete is high in lime, which is toxic to certain plants. Sweet potatoes, potatoes, tomatoes, capsicums, and strawberries are lime-hating and won't do well if exposed to lime. Of course, that doesn't mean that concrete containers are an absolute no-no. Many people use concrete containers for container gardening fruits and veggies, but it is essential to leach the container before planting your beloved fruit, veggies, and herbs.

You can leach a concreate container by watering it thoroughly a few times. Let the water drain away, and dry out before watering it again. This process will help to reduce the lime content. You can also leave the concrete container outside in the rain for a few weeks allowing the lime to leach out. Alternatively, when you buy a concrete container, ask if it has already been leached.

Because concrete containers are porous, you can expect to water your fruit, veggies, and herbs more frequently than using a plastic pot or grow bag. You may also find that concrete pots become stained outside due to the minerals and salts in the soil. You can, however, counteract this by painting the container with non-toxic, waterproof paint.

One of the great things about concrete containers is that they are available in extra-large sizes. They are also heavy, so they cant be blown over or bumped over easily.

METAL CONTAINERS & ENAMEL CONTAINERS

I have always liked the look of metal containers as they add a creative or arty element to any space. The upside of using metal containers is that they don't crack, chip, or break easily. However, they don't provide much insulation, resulting in the soil heating up quickly and drying out, which can be severely damaging to your plant's roots. You can overcome this problem by using hydromats or another form of insulation within the metal container. Insulation can also help to prevent your plant's roots from freezing during the cold months.

If an old metal container has caught your eye, make sure that it's not one of those old-fashioned ones that contain toxic lead. Make sure you're buying a container that's safe for your kids, pets, and of course, plants that you plan to consume.

Unfortunately, metal tends to rust. You won't get an entire lifetime out of your pot. It may rust gracefully, which adds to its appeal, but if you're looking for a "forever" container, metal isn't the best option.

Another point of interest is to ensure that the container has suitable drainage holes as metal is entirely non-porous and therefore offers no natural drainage whatsoever.

Keep in mind that some metal containers, especially cast iron ones, are hefty and may prove difficult to move once you've planted your fruit and veggies in them.

DIY CONTAINERS

Now, for the fun part! DIY containers are my favorite. You can get so creative with everyday items, and you can repurpose old containers, buckets, laundry baskets, bins, and more. I once planted succulents in old cups with holes drilled in the bottom and hung them on my fence line. Not only are they an attractive focal point, but I wasn't sending my old, outdated coffee mugs to a landfill.

Before looking at a list of some interesting DIY container ideas, I must warn you that there is a big downside to DIY containers. Unfortunately, these objects are not always made for plants, so there may be errors and failures along the way. For instance, an old wooden bucket may rot and fall apart in a few years, or your rusty wheel-less wheelbarrow repurposed for growing herbs may eventually rust through, leaving you with a bit of a problem on your hands. However, none of the few and far-between pitfalls have ever put me off. I love this artistic side of container gardening. I am sure you will too.

Below is a brief list of some of the items I have used for container gardening with much success.

- Old mugs for herbs
- Gumboots
- Drawers
- Veggie baskets
- Buckets
- Teapots
- Birdcage (great for herbs)
- Camping kettle

- Watering can
- Car tires
- Toolboxes
- Jugs
- Recycled fabric shopping bags

These are just some ideas – let your creative green thumb juices flow.

Now that you're thinking about what type of containers to gather for your container and grow bag experience, it's time to move onto the next chapter, which focuses on choosing the right veggies for your container and grow bag garden.

3

VEGETABLES FOR YOUR CONTAINER & GROW BAG GARDEN

Now that you've got the container and grow bag gardening mindset in place and you've chosen your pots, it's time to think about which vegetables to cultivate. It goes without saying that some vegetables do better than others in a container or grow bag. Some veggies need more space and have specific soil demands that perhaps aren't easy to replicate in a container/grow bag. However, certain plants love the confines of a pot, container, or grow bag and will provide you with many seasons of crops as thanks for your efforts.

Of course, when choosing which veggies and herbs to grow, it's not just about which vegetables will thrive in a container but also about the conditions you can provide. For instance, if you choose a vegetable that does well in a pot but demands full sun all day long when you only get a few hours of sun on your balcony, you're not going to feel as if you are winning. Choosing suitable vegetables that like containers and also do well in the type of conditions you can provide is the trick to a thriving container and grow bag garden.

This chapter is all about choosing the right veggies for your containers and grow bags. It is also about learning more on the following for each:

- Container size and spacing requirements
- Watering frequency
- Sunlight requirements (how much sun and for how many hours)
- Soil/growing medium requirements

VEGETABLES THAT THRIVE IN CONTAINER AND GROW BAG GARDENS

There are many vegetables to choose from for container gardening. However, for the sake of this book, I have decided to focus on my favorites! Here's a quick reference of the twelve vegetables we will cover in the pages to follow:

- Eggplant
- Peppers
- Tomato
- Squash
- Green Beans
- Lettuce
- Radishes
- Broccoli
- Turnip
- Spinach
- Cucumber

- Green Onions

Hopefully, these are on your list of favorite veggies too. Ready to learn more about how to grow these plants in a container or grow bag garden? Let's jump right in.

EGGPLANT (also called brinjal or aubergines)

Eggplants are perennial tropical vegetables that are native to China and India (South & East Asia. It's safe to say that eggplants are vegetables that go by many names. Some call them brinjals, and others call them aubergines. Whatever you choose to call them, I have some good news for you. Eggplants are a brilliant choice for container gardens and grow bags, and I recommend that you start with black beauty or purple varieties, as these have given me the best yield.

In fact, and this might be unique to me, but I have never had much success trying to grow them in the ground. As container plants on my balcony, they sprang into life and thrived. We love eating eggplant for breakfast, lunch, or dinner. You will find them packed with the goodness of vitamins B6, C, K, thiamine, niacin, manganese, phosphorus, magnesium, copper, folic acid, potassium. They are a great source of fiber too. Before I start waxing lyrical about eggplants, below is everything you need to know about creating their ideal growing conditions.

- **Pot Size**

One of the first things you need to know about eggplants is that they like their space. They don't like being bunched up with other plants. When eggplants are in a container, they need about 12 − 14 inches (30 − 45 cm) of space between them and other plants.

Obviously, you need a reasonably large container or grow bag for an eggplant as they can grow quite tall. A 5-gallon (18 l) container/grow bag is perfect. If you have a pot with a 20 inch (50 cm) diameter, you can safely plant three eggplants into it.

- **Watering Frequency**

I wouldn't go as far as to say eggplants are thirsty plants, but they do like frequent watering and don't like missing scheduled watering. When the weather is cool, you can give your eggplant around 1 inch (2.5 cm) water per week, but you should steadily increase this amount of water as the weather gets warmer. You can do this by lightly watering the top surface of the pot and then doing a finger test to estimate how much water is in the soil.

- **Sunlight Requirements**

Eggplants are sun worshipers. They do best when they have full sun for at least six hours per day. The more sun an eggplant has, the better it thrives. You will also find that your eggplant enjoys warmth. If it gets cold, it can take fright and may stop producing. Protect outdoor plants by bringing them indoors when the temperatures start to drop.

- **Soil Requirements**

You might begin to think that eggplants are luxurious plants. They like water, lots of sun, and, you guessed it, fertile nutrient-dense soil. If you aren't prepared to provide the luxuries it needs, you may never enjoy a decent crop from your plants. To provide your container eggplants with the ideal growing environment, add two parts good quality potting soil and one part of sand to the container. Combine these ingredients well before planting your eggplants.

PEPPERS (also called Capsicum)

Peppers are native to Central America, northern South America, and Mexico. This warm climate seasonal vegetable, also known as Capsicum, is called bell pepper in America or just pepper in the United Kingdom. I find it interesting that peppers form part of the Nightshade family, making them a close relative to eggplant, tomato, potato, petunia, and tobacco. You might think Nightshade plants are toxic, and some of them are. But, obviously, peppers and other veggies mentioned in this book are entirely safe to eat.

While there are more than 20 different types of pepper, there are only two varieties – hot or sweet. Peppers are an excellent vegetable for those who are all about health and nutrition. They are high in Vitamin A, C and potassium too. Best of all, they are super low in calories. When I say "low," I mean 22 calories per cup!

Many people choose peppers for their container and grow bag gardening project, and here's what you need to know about them to help them thrive.

- **Pot Size**

Pepper plants, like the eggplant, like their space. Peppers need about 12 inches (30 cm) of space around them when planted in a container or grow bag, which provides them with enough room to grow.

The size of the container or grow bag you use needs to be big enough to plant at least one or two pepper plants. Whether you're planning on planting hot peppers or sweet peppers, opt for a 5-gallon (18 l) container.

- **Watering Frequency**

Compared with other container and grow bag plants, peppers crave water. For peppers to produce quality blossoms and fruit, the soil must be moist, which means they require frequent watering. Drench the container or grow bag until the water drains out the drainage holes. Use a finger test to feel when the soil is drying out and when it is, water again.

- **Sunlight Requirements**

Peppers are warm climate seasonal vegetables, and they grow and produce when the air and soil temperatures are warm. You might have already guessed it, but peppers are sun-lovers. If you ever come across falling pepper blossoms, this is most likely due to a temperature change. Peppers will grow better and faster if you keep them relatively warm, night and day in the cold season.

- **Soil Requirements**

Peppers require warm soil that is well-fertilized as they are relatively heavy feeders. Aim to fertilize lightly every second week during the warmer months. Choose a time-release fertilizer to save you time and effort. Time-release fertilizers ensure that the peppers get constant nutrients for up to 4 months and reduces how often you need to fertilize.

TOMATO

I must admit that tomatoes are my favorite veggie to grow in containers and grow bags. I also find it fascinating that over 7,500 different types of tomatoes are out there in different shapes and sizes. Tomatoes are so versatile. You can add them to soups, stews, sauces, salads, pizzas, and even drinks.

Tomatoes originate from Central and South America and have become one of the most popular food crops globally. In addition, tomatoes are jam-packed with vitamins and minerals such as A, B1, B3, B6, C, E, and K, to name a few. In my mind, tomatoes are today's miracle food.

If you've chosen to grow tomatoes in containers and grow bags, firstly I must say "great choice, well done", and secondly, here's what you need to know about tomatoes to keep them healthy and happy.

- **Pot Size**

The type of tomato you choose to grow will play a role in the size container or grow bag you use. For instance, mini cherry tomatoes need a smaller pot than heirloom tomatoes. My favorite growing tomatoes are plum tomatoes, Campari tomatoes, and cherry tomatoes. My best advice to you is to pick the type of tomato you already enjoy eating.

Whatever you choose to grow, make sure you have a large container or grow bag, about 5-gallons (18 l) in-depth. Tomatoes require a decent amount of soil and need the space to develop strong roots to support the vine. Tomatoes love space and can become difficult to handle, maintain, and harvest if they are too close to each other. It's best to stick to one tomato plant per container or grow bag.

- **Watering Frequency**

A bit of good news is that tomatoes can be grown all year round. If you are planting tomatoes during warmer seasons, you should water your plants daily as heat can lead to wilting. If you're growing tomatoes in colder seasons, only water now and then when the soil starts to dry out. Again, make sure the soil is moist but never soggy. Remember to water the roots and not the plant, as wet tomato leaves are an attractive habitat for aphids, mites, and other destructive insects and diseases. Hold your hose onto the soil when watering and do the same with a watering can.

- **Sunlight Requirements**

Tomatoes thrive in full sun and need a minimum of 6 hours of sunlight a day. If your garden space is particularly hot and sunny, consider creating a semi-shade area for your tomatoes during the hottest time of the day. Too much sun can lead to the leaves and fruit scorching.

- **Soil Requirements**

Tomatoes planted in containers and grow bags need the soil to be at least 1 inch (2.5 cm) below the pot rim. This way, you can add a layer of mulch (straw, bark, chopped leaves) to help keep the soil moist. Try to add a cage or a tall stake for the tomatoes to climb over as they grow. It's best to plant the support cage (or stake) at the same time as the tomatoes. Inserting the support cage later may disrupt the tomatoes' growth and make them unhappy.

SQUASH

Squash originates in Central America and Mexico and comes in many shapes, sizes, and colors. When I first started growing squash, I discovered something quite interesting about them. Squash comes in two categories: summer squash and winter squash.

Summer squash (thin-skinned) has a quicker growth rate (60 days), while a winter squash (thick-skinned) takes some time (80 – 110 days). Types of summer squash include zucchini (most common) and pattypan. Winter squash consists of pumpkin, butternut, gem squash, and Hubbard. When it comes to choosing which squash to grow, my advice is to select the type of squash you regularly eat. Here's what you need to know about keeping squash plants happy in containers and grow bags.

- **Pot Size**

Squash makes for great container and grow bag plants. They thrive in containers/grow bags when the soil and environmental conditions are exactly right. You must choose a container or grow bag with a diameter of 24 inches (60 cm), and your container should be at least 12 inches deep (30 cm). One of the most important aspects of choosing a container for squash is drainage – so choose a container with sufficient drainage holes below. Only plant one squash plant per 5-gallon (18 l) container or grow bag.

- **Watering Frequency**

One unfortunate thing about squash plants is that they are prone to fungi and mold growth. If the soil is soggy or there is too much moisture around the plant, it will get mold, and then you're in trouble. Make sure that you don't wet the leaves when watering the plant. Try to direct the water only to the soil. For the first two weeks, you need to keep the soil moist, not dry, and not soggy either. After that, you can allow the soil to almost dry out before watering again.

- **Sunlight Requirements**

Squash adores the sun – in fact, I fondly refer to mine as my "little sun-worshippers". The more sunlight they get, the better they grow and produce, so don't try to place your squash containers and grow bags in a shady spot. Squash plants thrive on a full day of sunshine, but if you can't provide that, the absolute minimum amount of time they should be in the sun is 6 hours.

- **Soil Requirements**

Squash feed on soil that is rich in organic matter. The best way to ensure your soil is rich and nutritious is to use a time-release fertilizer. Add this to your soil the first time you plant your squash. Time-release fertilizers ensure that your plants get a boost of nutrients when they need it the most. This kind of fertilizer can last for up to four months, so it's well worth your investment. If you prefer to use a water-soluble fertilizer, make sure that you add it to your plant's container soil at least once every four weeks.

GREEN BEANS

Green beans originally come from Peru and, through migrating Indian tribes, soon spread throughout South and Central America. Green beans are a great vegetable choice for growing in containers and grow bags as they are simple and easy to grow. Green beans – also referred to as string beans – are a firm favorite on our dinner table. They are rich in Vitamins A, C, and K and are especially good for colon health.

There are two types of green beans you can grow. The bush green beans are quick and easy to grow, and the pole beans, which are runner beans, need a trellis for support. Green beans don't like the cold, so if you live in a cold part of the world, be prepared to bring your green beans indoors when the cold season strikes. Here's what you need to know to keep your green beans thriving in your container/grow bag garden.

- **Pot Size**

When I first started with growing green beans, I didn't realize how important it was to give them space. I recommend using a 2-gallon (14 l) size container or grow bag for green beans. If you are planting bush beans, then, ideally, you need to plant the seeds about 1 inch (2.5 cm) deep, 2 inches (5 cm) apart. Plant them in rows and make sure they are about 18 – 24 inches (45 – 60 cm) apart.

If you are planting pole/runner beans, remember that they will need a support structure (trellis) to support their growth. Make sure you build the support structures before you plant the seeds. Sow the seeds about 1 inch (2.5 cm) deep and 3 inches (8 cm) apart.

- **Watering Frequency**

Beans must be watered once or twice a week when the soil dries out. There's no need to keep the soil wet, but when the moisture leaves the soil, promptly water your beans so that they don't dry out. The best time to water your plant is in the morning. Try not to wet the leaves while watering as, much like squash plants, green beans are susceptible to fungal diseases.

- **Sunlight Requirements**

When growing green beans, make sure you choose a place that has a lot of sunshine. Green beans require about 8 hours of sunlight each day to thrive.

- **Soil Requirements**

Green beans grow best in slightly acidic to neutral soil. I found that clay or silt loamy soil is better for green bean production than sandy soils. Using a good compost and potting soil mix is perfect for green beans.

LETTUCE

Most people don't know that, and I find it fascinating, lettuce originally comes from Egypt. In Egypt (and in Greece, too), lettuce was used for its medicinal properties – they believed lettuce helped with sedation and digestion. Whether you want to grow lettuce for health reasons or simply want a filler in your salads and sandwich, one bit of good news is that lettuce is exceptionally easy to grow.

In addition, lettuce doesn't require a big container or grow bag, making it the perfect vegetable to grow even if you live in an apartment or have limited space. Here's what you need to know about lettuce if you wish to add it to your container or grow bag garden.

- **Pot Size**

I found that a 1-gallon (3.7 l) container is perfect for growing lettuce. Lettuce may not be space invaders above the soil, but they require ample room for root growth. Containers and grow bags that are 6 – 12 inches (15 – 30 cm) are ideal for growing several lettuce varieties. You can grow two plants in one container, and I strongly advise that you opt for loose-leaf lettuce as they are easier to grow in containers and grow bags than lettuce heads.

- **Watering Frequency**

It's probably ironic that while lettuce consists of mostly water, it does not enjoy soggy roots. Lightly water the soil around your lettuce as frequently as daily – do not drench the soil as this will take longer to dry out, and lettuce doesn't like that. Do not wet the leaves, and make sure that the container drains well.

- **Sunlight Requirements**

While lettuce enjoys sunlight, they aren't sun-worshippers. They only require around 4 – 6 hours of sunlight per day to thrive. If you only have a semi-shade area available for growing lettuce, they should do just fine.

- **Soil Requirements**

Lettuce enjoys soil with a pH of between 5.5 and 7. Planting lettuce in containers requires a quality soil mix that will retain water; you will need about 1 – 3½-gallons (7 – 13 l) of soil mix, depending on the pot size used. Regular potting soil is usually suitable for growing lettuce in containers and grow bags.

RADISHES

I have always been a fan of radishes and find it interesting that they originate from China. When they spread globally, they became a prominent food choice in Rome, Greece, and Egypt.

Some records show radishes were served as part of meals long before the Egyptian pyramids were constructed!

Radishes, which are available in many different colors and sizes, are a firm favorite grown globally. What's more is that they thrive in containers and grow bags, producing in as little as 23 days.

Here's what you need to know about radishes if you choose to grow them in containers and grow bags.

- **Pot Size**

Radishes don't need a lot of space to thrive. In fact, a 1-gallon (3.7 l) container or grow bag is all you need to grow 3 radishes. Although radishes are relatively small, you still need to ensure that your container or grow bag has good depth. Enough surrounding space will ensure that the roots can form correctly. Alternatively, if you're growing baby radishes, you can use a standard 12 inch (30 cm) flowerpot to produce a dozen radishes. If you're starting from seed, it would be best to plant each radish seed 1 inch (2.5 cm) below the surface and 1 inch (2.5 cm) apart.

- **Watering Frequency**

Radishes thrive in soil that is moist but not soggy. Well-watered seeds should germinate within 5 – 10 days. Keep the soil moist by watering your radishes every other day. Once your seedlings sprout, you can reduce watering to 2 or 3 times per week, but only when the soil starts drying out. Note that I said, "starts drying out". If you allow the soil to dry out completely between watering, the roots may start to crack, which doesn't bode well for your radish crop.

- **Sunlight Requirements**

An adequate amount of sunlight will ensure that your radish roots grow quickly and healthily. Radishes aren't particularly demanding in terms of sunlight, but for the best health of your plants, ensure that they get at least 6 hours of direct sunlight per day. You can grow radishes in partial sun of $4 - 5$ hours per day, but growth may be slightly slower.

- **Soil Requirements**

Radishes can be quite fussy when it comes to soil. They like nutrient-rich soil that drains well and is permeable. There should be no obstruction to root growth, so ensure that your potting mix is fine or opt to make your own. If you make your own soil, opt for a loamy soil as they aren't fond of clay soils and keep the soil free from rocks and stones. Add a cup or two of compost or well-rotted manure to your potting mix when first planting your radishes to give them a growing boost.

BROCCOLI

I adore broccoli. We always have it freshly steamed and ready on our dinner table, and sometimes I can't help but marvel over how many attractive variants there are. In general, broccoli is native to the eastern Mediterranean and Asia Minor. It was quite a popular crop in ancient Roman times, and it's interesting to note that it only made its way into the UK and USA in the early 1700s.

Choosing broccoli for your container or grow bag garden is a fine choice as it's easy to grow and highly nutritious. Broccoli is a good source of iron, potassium, selenium, calcium, magnesium, and vitamins A, E, C, B, and K.

You will find that it's not particularly fussy – even if it's got a poor soil choice, and this is the reason why it is most newbie container gardeners' number 1 choice!

Belstar, Calabrese, and Destiny varieties are the most commonly seen in the grocery store. If you want to branch out and try to grow something a little more interesting, I highly recommend you try your hand at growing Purple Sprouting broccoli which is cold-hardy by the way, and Romanesco that is stunning with its peaks and creative shapes (this is definitely one worth looking up). You can see a variety of broccoli types here: https://gardenerspath.com/plants/vegetables/best-broccoli-varieties

If you choose to grow broccoli in containers or grow bags, here's what you need to know about keeping them comfortable and thriving.

- **Pot Size**

I would recommend a 5-gallon (18 l) container or grow bag for growing broccoli. Broccoli gets comprehensive coverage so planting one in a 5-gallon pot is ideal. You can plant the seeds directly in your container, or you could start to harden off your seedlings indoors and transplant them when they are sturdy seedlings. Hardening off your seedlings exposes your seedlings gradually to outside conditions until they are big enough to be planted in the appropriate temperatures. If you want to group your broccoli, you can comfortably grow three broccoli plants in a 15-gallon (57 l) container.

- **Watering Frequency**

Broccoli requires regular watering. You can drench the soil until the water runs out of the drainage holes. Only water again when the soil starts to dry out. If you live in a temperate climate, you should only need to water your broccoli twice a week, maybe three times.

• Sunlight Requirements

Broccoli needs 6 hours of sunlight at most. While it likes a few hours of sun, it's important to note that broccoli is sensitive to temperature. They do best in a semi-sun environment that gets some shade each day. If you are growing broccoli from seed, it's good to know that the ideal germinating temperature for them is 75 – 80 F (23 – 27 C). If it's too hot outside, broccoli seeds may never sprout.

Also, because broccoli is a partial shade plant, you should avoid using a black container as black attracts and traps the sun's heat. You may feel tempted to keep your broccoli in the shade because it is so sensitive to heat, but don't do that! If your broccoli is sun-starved, it will grow thin spindly stems and a small or deformed head.

You can use a mulch to keep your broccoli cool if it's a hot summer or you live in a hot climate. Mulching is critical to growing broccoli. Organic mulch will cool the soil down by about 4 – 6 degrees F (14 degrees C). The ideal mulch is achieved by spreading a 2 – 4 inch (5 – 10 cm) layer of chopped leaves, hay, and straw on the soil's surface as the broccoli stems grow.

• Soil Requirements

Broccoli prefers slightly acidic soil. When creating soil for the container or grow bag, keep in mind that they like well-drained, moisture-retentive soil with a texture somewhere between clay loam and sandy. Ensure that your soil has plenty of organic matter, and add a nitrogen-rich fertilizer in moderation to keep your broccoli happy.

. . .

TURNIPS

Turnips are a fabulous all-rounder and originate from middle and Eastern Asia. Their leaves taste delicious in salads or even in pasta dishes, and you can use the bulbs in place of potatoes. They also make great pickles, in case you didn't know. Turnips are rich in nutrients and low in calories.

They are packed with vitamins B6 and C, folate, calcium, copper, potassium, manganese, and dietary fiber. When turnips are 2 – 3 inches (5 – 8 cm) in diameter, they are ready to be harvested. If you leave them for too long, they will mature and become firm and feel woody.

While people use the enormous variety of turnips as livestock feed, they're a popular dinner-table favorite for many. Here's what you need to know about turnips if you choose to grow them in containers and grow bags.

- **Pot Size**

I recommend using a 2-gallon container (14 l) with at least 12 inches (30 cm) depth when growing turnips. A 2-gallon (14 l) container or grow bag will comfortably grow two turnips at a time. Pay special attention to the type of container you use. You can use glazed ceramic, plastic, or terracotta pots, but you need to ensure that your container has suitable drainage holes. Turnips are prone to root rot, so a container that drains well is essential. Using a coffee filter at the bottom of your pot is a smart way to prevent soil from being washed out of the draining holes when you water your plant.

- **Watering Frequency**

Turnips don't demand water, but they do need regular watering. Before watering your turnips, poke your finger into the soil to check how dry it is. Only water your turnips when the top $1/2 - 1$ inch $(1 - 2$ cm$)$ of soil is dry. Soak the soil until the water starts to drain through the drainage holes. Wilting leaves are an indication that your plant needs more water.

If you're in a dry region with less rainfall, then soak your turnips well by watering them $2 - 3$ times a week. In addition to watering your turnips as required, you need moisture-rich soil. The moisture in the soil will prevent your turnips from becoming tough and developing a bitter taste (if you've had bitter turnips before, now you know why!).

- **Sunlight Requirements**

Turnips adore the sun, so do them a favor by positioning them in a very sunny spot. They enjoy around 6 hours of full sun per day. However, if your container garden lacks full sunlight, it's not a train-smash as turnips will tolerate partial shade too.

- **Soil Requirements**

Turnips have similar soil requirements to radishes. They enjoy permeable, well-draining soil that offers no root growth obstruction. You can use a good quality potting mix or make your own, ensuring that it's more loamy than clay, is fine, and has no stones. Adding $1 - 2$ cups of compost or well-rotted manure will also keep your turnips very happy.

SPINACH

I find it interesting that spinach originates from Persia (that's Iran now, by the way). Originally, it was known as "aspanakh". However, it only entered China in the 7th century when the

King of Nepal sent it as a gift. It later started working its way into the Western world and was a popular veggie in the USA in the early 19th century.

Spinach is a firm favorite on many dinner tables and container gardens too. Spinach is considered somewhat of a super-food as it's rich in potassium, magnesium, carotenoids, which are antioxidants, folic acid, iron, calcium, and vitamins B6, B9, C, and K.

I find it's one of the easier vegetables to grow as they spring up quickly and are generally quite hardy. However, a few Asian varieties grow slowly and are more suitable for growing in a hot and humid climate. Spinach doesn't need special care when grown in a pot. I recommend looking out for the semi-savoy variety as they are easier to grow, hardy, and relatively disease resistant.

- **Pot Size**

When you're scouting for a container or grow bag for your spinach, I'd recommend a wide container rather than a deep one. You can even opt for several small pots or a wooden crate. Size-wise, a 1-gallon (3.7 l) container will support two plants comfortably.

Each spinach plant needs a space of 3 inches (8 cm). If you are keen to grow large and sturdy leaves, leaving about 5 inches (12.7 cm) between plants for growing. If you're planning to harvest your plants early as baby spinach, you can space the plants out 2 inches (5 cm) apart.

- **Watering Frequency**

Spinach is a really heavy drinker, so it's essential to keep the soil moist but not soggy. I would recommend watering daily in the warm season and checking to see if the soil is still damp before watering in the cold season. The soil should always be moist – don't let it dry out between watering. If you happen to overwater the spinach or your water is not draining out well, you must drain out stagnant water, otherwise the plant may rot or catch a fungal disease. As with all vegetables, avoid wetting the leaves when watering.

- **Sunlight Requirements**

If you're growing spinach in a mild climate, choose a sunny spot for your spinach. However, if you're living in a warmer climate, you need to avoid overheating your plant as spinach is quite heat sensitive. You know it is getting too much sun if it is well-watered but still wilting. While spinach does well in 6 hours of moderate heat full sun each day, it will still be happy and thrive with around 3 – 4 hours of sunlight.

- **Soil Requirements**

When growing spinach in containers and grow bags, ensure you use a quality potting soil mix rich in organic matter. Spinach thoroughly enjoys a crumbly and loamy soil texture. Soil that waterlogs or clogs is unacceptable for spinach under any circumstances. Well-draining soil is an absolute must, and it's a good idea to ensure that the pH of the soil is neutral too.

CUCUMBER

Cucumbers have a fascinating history – for me at least. While they originate from India, between the Bay of Bengal and the Himalayan Mountains, research shows that they were grown and eaten in ancient Egypt some 3,000 years ago! Christopher

Columbus took cucumbers into America in the late 1400s, and soon they spread across the world.

Of course, it's not just the history of cucumbers that makes them a popular choice for grow bag and container growing. Cucumbers taste good, are a healthy food option, and are packed with vitamins B, C, K, copper, potassium, phosphorus, and magnesium.

Cucumbers have sprawling vines that you can train to grow upwards on a trellis, which I quite like about them. One unfortunate thing is that cucumbers can be challenging to grow. You'll need to be selective about the cucumbers you opt to plant.

I recommend planting the Picolino F1 cucumber. These mini cucumbers are compact and reach about 4 – 5 inches (12 – 14 cm). These cucumbers are relatively easy to grow and provide a beautiful sweet flavor. The Saber F1 and Parisi F1 cucumbers reach 8 – 9 inches (20 – 22 cm) and will give a good yield. Another good choice is the H-19 Little Leaf and National Pickling cucumbers. They grow relatively quickly, are both pickling cucumbers, and are great for snacking on. My children love these in their lunch boxes!

- **Pot Size**

When growing cucumbers, I recommend using a 1-gallon (3.7 l) container for each plant. Your container will need depth so that your cucumbers can develop an extensive root system if you want an abundant yield. One thing to be aware of is that cumbers do not transplant very well. If you are transplanting a seedling to a bigger pot, I recommend using a biodegradable cup at first (plant the cup into the bigger pot) as cucumbers are prone to shock. I strongly recommend planting your seeds directly into the container you're going to be growing them in.

- **Watering Frequency**

Cucumber plants photosynthesize during the day and release water through transpiration. For this reason, it's best to water your cucumbers in the morning, provided it's not going to rain later on. Your cucumbers will require 1 inch (2.5 cm) of water every week. It would be best to check the moisture of the soil using your finger before watering. If your soil is dry, water thoroughly. If your soil is wet, don't water it again until it becomes dry on the surface. You'll want your soil to retain moisture just below the surface, so the soil you use is quite important.

- **Sunlight Requirements**

Cucumbers like around 5 hours of sunlight each day, so place your container or grow bag in a sunny spot. It's good to know that as warm weather plants, it's best to initially plant them when the weather is warm.

- **Soil Requirements**

Cucumbers thrive in loose sandy loam soil, but even so, you will find that they do well in any well-draining soil. Your cucumber plant's roots will grow around 36 – 48 inches (90 – 120 cm) deep, so it's a good idea to provide sufficient soil to support this. I recommend sowing your seeds into peat-free, multi-purpose compost. You can get good quality potting soil that retains moisture at the local garden center. While I did say that cucumbers will do well in any well-draining soil, avoid using garden soil as this doesn't drain as well as potting soil mixes and may be plagued with insects and diseases – something to which cucumbers are sensitive.

. . .

GREEN ONIONS

Green onions are thought to be native to Asia and have been cultivated for over 2,000 years! Green onions are one of my top recommendations for newbie container and grow bag gardeners because they're easy to grow and aren't susceptible to pests or diseases. Green onions are different from scallions and spring onions and are packed with beta-carotene, calcium, folate, and vitamins A and C. Green onions find their way into nearly every meal in my home.

Their green shoots are perfect for garnishing your food or including them as part of your salad, and better still, you can grow green onions all year round. The best time to plant them is in spring if you're in a cold climate. If, however, your region is much warmer, anytime will do.

If you want some instant gratification, I don't recommend growing green onions from seed as they can take a while to sprout and genuinely start to shine. Instead, opt to grow seedlings you can get from the local garden center. When you buy green onions from your local grocery store, don't throw away the roots. Keep them along with 1 inch (2.5 cm) of the green leaves still intact as you can pop them in soil and watch them grow. Green onions are a re-harvesting delight. Simply snip the shoots close to the soil, and they will regrow over and over. Here's what you need to know about planting green onions in containers and grow bags.

- **Pot Size**

A 1-gallon (3.7 l) container or grow bag can comfortably house 3 – 5 green onion bulbs. You can plant your bulbs by placing them in the pot root side down. Cover only half of the bulb with 2 inches (5 cm) of soil. Leave the green shoot and the top half of the bulb above the ground. Ensure that your bulbs are spaced 1.5 – 2 inches (4 – 5 cm) apart.

- **Watering Frequency**

When growing green onions in containers and grow bags, the soil needs to be well-watered and evenly moist at all times. While it's good to water your bulbs regularly, try not to overdo it as onions do not enjoy soggy soil. You will find that they need around 2 – 3 inches (5 – 7 cm) water per week and a bit more when the weather is hot. It's a good idea to check your onions daily by touching the top of the soil. If the soil's surface is dry, it's time to give them a bit of water.

- **Sunlight Needed**

Your green onions will flourish when they have 6 – 7 hours of sunlight per day. If you're growing them indoors, leave them at a bright window that provides direct sunlight. Green onions love the sun and enjoy warm climates, so you may have to protect them when the colder months come around.

- **Soil Requirements**

I find green onions grow best when I use an organic soil mix, but that said, I have also seen them thrive in just about any type of well-draining soil. Onions enjoy nutrient-rich soil, so I always add compost into the soil before planting my onions. You should work organic matter into the soil at least 6 – 8 inches (15 – 20 cm) deep and ensure no stones could get in the way of the root growth.

4

FRUITS FOR YOUR CONTAINER & GROW BAG GARDEN

One of the best things about growing fruit in containers and grow bags is that you get to enjoy fruit exposed to fewer or no toxic chemicals and pesticides. Of course, you're not going to have the same yield as your grocery store suppliers do, but your plants should be able to grow enough fruit to serve your family, and that's the most rewarding part!

When growing fruit in containers, it's best to familiarize yourself with the growing conditions they most enjoy. Knowing these tidbits of information will take your container garden's yield to the next level.

In this chapter will learn more about each of my favorite container and grow bag fruits in terms of:

- Container size and spacing requirements
- Watering frequency
- Sunlight requirements (how much sun and for how many hours)
- Soil/growing medium requirements

I have carefully selected fruits that I know do well in grow bags and containers. I have had much success with these fruits and feel they are great options to get newbie container gardeners started.

Here's a quick look at the fruits we will be focusing on:

- Apples
- Blueberries
- Cherries
- Figs
- Peaches and Nectarines
- Plums
- Raspberries
- Strawberries

Throughout this chapter, you will notice that there's an inch (cm) measurement for watering each plant in the "Watering Frequency" section. This refers to the amount of water a plant needs regarding rainfall read in a rain gauge. In all instances, container plants require a full pot drenching and should be watered again when the surface soil starts to dry out. I strongly recommend starting a booklet that records each of your container plants' water consumption rate. For instance, you may mark down that your apples tend to need water every ten days, and your blueberries need water every six days. Make a note and set a reminder on your mobile phone so that you don't miss important watering days.

Let's jump right into learning more about each fruit and what they require.

APPLES

The apple tree originates from Central Asia. In fact, its wild ancestor, called Malus Sieversii, still grows there today. Apples have grown in Asia and Europe for thousands of years, and it's thought that European colonists were responsible for taking apples to North America!

Apples are a nutritious and healthy addition to any diet, that's for sure. They make for a great crunchy snack or crispy addition to breakfast cereal in my home. And if you didn't know already, apples contain a powerful flavonoid called quercetin which boosts the immune system. A healthy immune system is crucial to the health of your entire body.

In addition to this, apples are good for digestion, eliminate toxins from the body, and are a great source of vitamin B6, K, potassium, copper, and manganese.

To keep apples happy and producing, here's what you need to know.

- **Pot Size**

When growing apples, you need to use a container or grow bag that's at least 5 – 6 gallons big (18 – 22 l) and about 12 inches (30 cm) deep. Don't go for a large container or grow bag right from the start, as it can stunt your tree's overall growth. Instead, start growing your tree in a small container and work your way up. As the tree grows, you will need to transplant it into bigger containers annually, which allows your fruit tree to "grow into the pot", ensuring it develops steadily and healthily.

- **Watering Frequency**

Like other fruit trees, apple trees must be watered regularly if there's no natural rainfall. If you get regular rainfall, there's no real need to water your apple tree. When watering your tree, soak the soil and only re-water every ten days or so. Apples require 1 inch or (2.5 cm) of water per week.

If you see your apple tree in its flowering stage, you may increase the watering rate slightly. However, when the tree is dormant in winter, reduce the amount of watering. The rule of thumb when it comes to watering apple trees is to do the finger test. Simply poke your index finger into the container's soil, and if the top few inches are dry, it's time to water your tree. Don't overdo it.

- **Sunlight Requirements**

Apple trees are robust, but something I learned the hard way is that they don't like to get too hot or too cold. Starting with this knowledge will save you a lot of heartache in the long run. Apple trees thrive in moderate climates, so it's a good idea to do your best to provide them with the correct positioning on your balcony, porch, or garden. Provide your apple tree with 6 hours of sunlight or 8 – 10 hours of dappled light, and it should be happy!

- **Soil Requirements**

Apple trees aren't too fussy when it comes to soil *type*. I have found they will grow happily in most soil textures, acidity, and structure. They do, however, demand that the soil is fertile and well-draining. I have grown my apple trees in medium-clay to sandy loam soil with great success.

Since apples are big consumers of nutrients, you will need to fertilize them, especially when they are young and in the beginning stages of growth. Feed your apple tree with a half-strength liquid fertilizer every two weeks while the tree is young. When your apple tree has matured, it's time to switch to a fruit tree fertilizer. Remember to reduce the amount of fertilizer used when you enter fall as your tree's growth phase slows down. You don't need to fertilize your tree at all in winter.

BLUEBERRIES

Blueberries, native to North America, are an excellent choice for container and grow bag gardens. Blueberries are a firm favorite in my home. Blueberries happen to be a brilliant source of manganese, vitamin C, and vitamin K and also have small amounts of vitamin B6, E, and copper.

They're great for topping cereals, pancakes, yogurts, and waffles. I also enjoy folding them into sweet bread and muffins or blending them into a nutritious smoothie. In addition, blueberries have an excellent reputation for fighting cancer, supporting heart health, increasing bone strength, and keeping skin healthy. If you choose to grow blueberries, here's what you need to know to keep them happy and thriving.

- **Pot Size**

Blueberries are pretty sensitive to the container or grow bag size. If you use a container that's too big, it could slow down or stunt your plant's growth. If you choose a container or grow bag that is too small, it could weaken and stunt the existing root system, which means a poor yield, unfortunately.

Choose a container or grow bag at least 12 – 18 inches (30 – 46 cm) deep. Opt for a container that is at least 12 inches (30 cm) wide for 1 blueberry bush. I grow my blueberries in crates because they like to spread horizontally. The more space you give them for growth, the happier they will be and the better the yield will be too!

- **Watering Frequency**

Blueberries don't like to be kept waiting for water, so I recommend developing a watering schedule and sticking to it, which requires you to get to know your blueberry plants. I set a reminder on my mobile phone just in case I get busy and forget. Blueberries need around 1 inch (2.5 cm) of water each week during the cooler months and about 4 inches (10 cm) of water during the growing and harvesting seasons.

Blueberries don't tolerate soggy roots, so drench the container or grow bag thoroughly when watering, but don't allow it to remain waterlogged. Make sure that you use well-draining soil and a grow bag or container that drains well too.

- **Sunlight Requirements**

You will find that blueberries are sun lovers. They don't do well when kept in the shade, so choose a sunny spot for your blueberries. You should provide your plant with at least 6 – 8 hours of full sun each day.

- **Soil Requirements**

Blueberries enjoy sandy soil that's fertilized regularly. Any acidic fertilizer for edible crops will work fine. If you're looking for a generous yield of blueberries, then fertilize and use compost regularly, being careful not to over-fertilize, and always follow the instructions on the package. Remember that blueberry shrubs need to be kept moist, so add some mulch to the top of your soil to help the container or grow bag retain some moisture.

CHERRIES

What I find fascinating about cherries, over and above their fantastic smell and flavor, is that they are part of the rose family. Cherries originally come from Asia Minor, somewhere between the Black Sea and the Caspian Sea. Rumor has it that the fruit spread into other countries by birds. The Greeks were the first nation to cultivate and produce cherries on a large scale.

Like the blueberries, cherries can be folded and baked into biscuits and pies, blended into smoothies, added to cereals, or paired with herbs and meats. The cherry is considered a low-calorie fruit packed with powerful antioxidants responsible for reducing inflammation, eliminating toxins, and relieving pain in the body. In addition to this, they are packed with vitamins A, C, and K, along with potassium, calcium, and magnesium. Who knew such a healthy snack could be so nutritional.

If you're ready to start growing cherries in containers and grow bags, here's what you need to know about helping them grow and thrive:

- **Pot Size**

Cherry trees require large garden containers or grow bags - about 15-gallon (56 l) deep. Choose a wide container or grow bag and ensure that it has sufficient drainage holes. A single grow bag is perfect for planting a self-pollinating tree (sour/tart cherries). If you plant a cherry tree that is not self-pollinating (sweet cherries), you will need a second tree and a second container too.

- **Watering Frequency**

Even though cherries enjoy water, they don't need to be watered too frequently. Watering your cherry tree once every 7 – 10 days or even once every second week is more than enough. Of course, if you stay in a dry and hot area and notice your cherry tree container soil is drying out quickly, you may have to water more frequently. When watering your cherry tree, soak the soil entirely until the water is draining out of the container/grow bag. While watering, keep the stream of water away from the fruit. Unfortunately, if you keep wetting cherries while watering, the fruit will begin to split.

- **Sunlight Requirements**

You must give them sufficient sunlight for your cherry trees to produce a good yield. Your cherries will enjoy around 8 hours of full sun per day. Because they are so demanding of sunlight, don't allow other plants to cast a shadow on them. In fact, you should find the sunniest spot to position your cherry containers/grow bags.

- **Soil Requirements**

Cherry trees are fans of light, sandy soil. They also thoroughly enjoy organic fertilizer (I use seaweed fertilizer) and will give you a bountiful yield if you use it regularly. If you want your cherry trees to thrive, avoid using nitrogen-heavy fertilizers as they don't respond well to it. To keep the soil moist, use mulch on the top layer of soil.

. . .

FIGS

One fruit I adore growing is figs. Figs originate from Northern Asia Minor and only made their way into California in the 1820s. Figs are a fruit known for their positive probiotic impact on the gut while being jam-packed with antioxidants, calcium, copper, and vitamin B6.

If you're looking for a fast-growing fruit, figs are it. Just keep in mind that figs prefer to be brought inside during the cold season.

Here's what you need to know if you want to keep your container figs healthy and happy.

- **Pot Size**

When starting with a fig seedling, it's best to plant it in a small grow bag or container. Then, keep transplanting your fig tree into a bigger container or grow bag as it grows. Your first pot should be around 5 – 7-gallons (18 – 26 l) deep.

- **Watering Frequency**

Figs enjoy regular watering of 1 – 1.5 inches (2.5 – 4 cm) each week. Figs don't enjoy drying out entirely between watering, so keep an eye on the moisture levels in the soil. Figs leaves tend to turn yellow and drop if overwatered.

- **Sunlight Requirements**

Figs love warm climates, and as such, it's essential to provide your tree with around 8 hours of sunlight per day. As noted earlier, if you plan on growing fig trees in containers, be prepared to move them indoors during the colder months as this is when your tree's roots are dormant, and your tree will prefer a warmer, draft-free environment.

- **Soil Requirements**

Fig trees aren't too demanding when it comes to soil. Of course, they prefer well-draining soil but will thrive in most soil types, even low fertility and heavy clay soils. If you want your tree to thrive, provide it with soil rich in organic matter. You can fertilize your fig tree once each year with a general-purpose fertilizer. It's best to fertilize a little at a time as they can be sensitive to overfertilizing.

PEACHES AND NECTARINES

Peaches and nectarines make for delicious snacks or sweet treats. You will find these fruits pretty nutritious, too, as they offer vitamin C, A, and potassium. Both peaches and nectarines are native to China and probably made it onto the scene around 2,000 years ago. They were popular crops in Persia, Rome, and Greece. And, of course, they are a vastly popular crop across the globe today. If you are interested in growing peaches and nectarines in containers and grow bags, I recommend looking out for a natural dwarf variant as they thrive in containers.

Here are a few tidbits of advice to ensure your peaches and nectarines are healthy and thriving.

- **Pot Size**

Keep in mind that most dwarf peach and nectarine trees will grow to around 6 ft (2 m) tall. With this knowledge, you can set about choosing the right size container or grow bag you need at each phase of your tree's growing process. A 5-gallon

(18 l) container or grow bag is ideal for one peach or nectarine tree.

Good drainage is vitally important when selecting a container by simply ensuring there are sufficient drainage holes at the bottom. As the tree matures, you will need to re-pot it in a larger container (transplant during the winter as your tree's roots are dormant during this time) each year.

- **Watering Frequency**

Your peach/nectarine tree needs a generous amount of water when you first plant it. You can water your plant deeply until it flows from the drainage holes. After that, water when the soil feels dry 2 inches (5 cm) below the surface do a simple finger test.

- **Sunlight Requirements**

Peach and nectarine trees are sun lovers. While they enjoy 8 hours of sun each day, they will also thrive if they can only get 6. When you bring your tree indoors during the colder months, set the pot near a sunny window so that it can get its sunshine fix.

- **Soil Requirements**

Peach and nectarine trees will thrive if you give them loamy soil with a generous amount of organic compost mixed in. Always ensure that if your tree has a graft line, it must not be buried beneath the soil and must be visible above the surface of the soil. To ensure that your peach and nectarine trees have good flower and fruit production, use a phosphorus-based fertilizer twice per year.

. . .

PLUMS

Fresh, sweet, succulent plums are another favorite in my home. When we have plums growing, you can almost feel everyone's anticipation for harvest day! The history books tell us that plums originated in China around 470 BC.

They're a great on-the-go snack and are excellent in sauces, puddings, pies, and tarts. You will find more than 15 vitamins and minerals in plums, including calcium, phosphorus, magnesium, folate, and vitamins A, C, and K.

If you choose to grow plums in containers and grow bags, here's what you need to know about keeping them happy.

- **Pot Size**

Plums require a container or grow bag size that's 20 inches (50 cm) or wider to thrive. It's best to start with this size and work your way up to a bigger container/grow bag as your tree grows. Ensure that your chosen container offers sufficient drainage.

One of the best things about plums grown in containers and grow bags is that they don't grow particularly big, so you won't have to struggle with pruning and should be able to move it around in its container with relative ease.

- **Watering Frequency**

Plums are very thirsty plants and need to be watered weekly. When there's no rain, soak the entire container until the water starts to seep through the drainage holes. You need to maintain moist soil down to around 24 inches (60 cm) below the soil's surface. Ensure that your tree's soil is moist to this level and don't allow it to dry out. If you do, your tree will start to wilt, and your fruit yield will be far from impressive and possibly even non-existent.

- **Sunlight Requirements**

Plum trees adore sunshine, so aim to provide it around 8 hours of full sun per day. If you have a sunny deck or balcony, position your pot there and watch it thrive. As sun-loving plants, plum trees do not like to get cold, so be prepared to move them indoors during the colder months (an unheated shed or garage will be fine).

- **Soil Requirements**

Plum trees like well-drained, loamy soil. Keep in mind that plums like soil with a pH level of 5.0 − 6.5. They also enjoy fertilizer, which you can add to the soil in early spring, and you can use a balanced general fertilizer for this. If you're going the organic route, you can fertilize with dried poultry manure pellets and organic potassium. Fertilize once in the first year of life and then twice a year after that.

RASPBERRIES

Raspberries are said to originate from eastern Asia, while others believe they are native to Europe. One thing I know for sure is that they are one of my favorite fruits to grow. I find them a playful fruit and enjoy turning them into jam and sauces. My family also thoroughly enjoys them as a straight-from-the-tree snack. Interestingly enough, you can also use raspberry leaves to make tea.

One thing to note is that some raspberries grow pretty big, and I would not recommend trying to grow them in a container or grow bag. For this reason, I recommend looking for dwarf, thornless varieties such as the Heritage or Raspberry Shortcake.

If raspberries are on your shortlist of plants for your container or grow bag garden, here's everything you should know about growing and nurturing them.

- **Pot Size**

Each raspberry plant will enjoy having its own space. For sizable plants with a generous yield, you need a container or grow bag that is at least 24 inches (about 60 cm) wide and 36 inches (90 cm) deep.

- **Watering Frequency**

Raspberries aren't very thirsty plants but will still require some water each week. You should aim to give your plant around 1 – 1.5 inches (2.5 – 5 cm) of water at a time. Keeping the soil moist is quite important. If you notice that the soil is starting to dry out, it's time to water your raspberries. Never allow the container soil to dry out completely between watering.

- **Sunlight Requirements**

Raspberries are sun worshippers and require at least 6 – 8 hours of full sun per day. If your raspberries are in partial shade, however, they will still thrive and produce. When winter comes around, your raspberries will go into their dormant phase. It's best to move your raspberries indoors and out of the cold when the cold months approach.

- **Soil Requirements**

You don't have to create anything special for raspberries in terms of soil. Instead, purchase a good quality potting soil mix, and your plants will be happy. You can also add some organic fertilizer every spring to give your raspberries a well-deserved boost.

STRAWBERRIES

What I find the most fascinating about strawberries is that their seeds are on full display on the outside! What's even more astounding is that strawberries are so well-loved that around nine million tonnes are produced each year. Strawberries are mentioned in ancient Roman literature as a medicinal plant, and the French began growing and harvesting the fruit in the fourteenth century.

Strawberries are a good source of manganese, potassium, folate, and vitamin C. Strawberries are delicious when plucked straight from the plant. You can also work them into desserts, smoothies, jams, or eat them coated in the likes of cream, chocolate, or yogurt.

Here's what you need to know about growing and nurturing strawberries in pots and containers.

- **Pot Size**

No matter how small your space is, strawberries will enjoy your balcony in a grow bag, the usual terracotta pot, or even a hanging basket. Whatever container you choose, make sure it's 18 inches (46 cm) wide and 8 inches (20 cm) deep with several drainage holes.

Containers are great for growing strawberries as they keep pests like slugs and snails at bay. You should keep an eye out for hungry birds and protect your strawberries by placing a loose net over them. Most people want to get terracotta pots because they look great. A plastic pot, however, will help the soil retain moisture. A plastic pot inside a terracotta pot will work well if you want the best of both worlds.

- **Watering Frequency**

Giving your strawberries a small amount of water each day will help them to produce a thriving yield. Strawberries need around 1 − 2 inches (3 − 5 cm) of water each week. Before watering your strawberries, do a simple finger test. Poke your index finger around 1 inch (2.5 cm) into the soil. If the soil is moist, let it be. If the first inch of soil is dry, you can water your plants again.

Avoid wetting the fruit and leaves as this can attract insect infestations and diseases. Strawberries enjoy warm climates and typically become dormant during the winter. As a result, be prepared to move them indoors or undercover during the winter months.

- **Sunlight Requirements**

Strawberries do their best work when positioned in a sunny spot. They thrive on around 6 − 8 hours of full sun per day. The only time you should consider moving your strawberries into dappled light or part shade is when the strawberries are ripening. Don't pluck the strawberries off the plant until they are ripe, as unripe harvested strawberries don't ripen.

- **Soil Requirements**

Strawberries do best in a blend of compost and a high-quality potting mix. You can mix both in equal parts before planting your strawberries. Bare root runners need to be soaked in a bucket of water if they are looking dull. Allow the roots to penetrate the full depth of your container. You can plant them so that the crown is just above the surface. Alternatively, purchasing regular pot-sold strawberries will give you a head start to grow your strawberries.

5

HERBS FOR YOUR CONTAINER AND GROW BAG GARDEN

One of my favorite things to grow in containers and grow bags is herbs. I find it most rewarding to nip outside to grab a few handfuls of Basil and Rocket when making a zesty salad. I also thoroughly enjoy adding generous helpings of Rosemary and Thyme to hearty stews and saucy dishes.

Of course, you can do a lot more with herbs. They are so versatile that you can use the same herbs on a pizza and in a chicken a la king. I also found that because they grow so quickly, my kids love to get involved in caring for and maintaining my containers and grow bags of herbs.

To provide you with the best advice that I have gleaned over the years, I am focusing this chapter on how to grow and garden my favorite selection of herbs. If you can master these, and I know you can, you should move on to trying some of *your* favorite herbs too.

Here's a sneak peek at the herbs you will be learning more about in this section:

- Parsley
- Basil
- Greek Oregano
- Rosemary
- Thyme
- Mint
- Lemon balm

Ready to get started? Let's jump right in!

PARSLEY

Most people don't know this, but Parsley is one of the most potent disease-fighting plants out there. This beautiful flowering plant is said to have originated in the Mediterranean region of southern Europe and western Asia. You can use Parsely as a fragrant herb in stews, sauces, vegetables, rice, and fish dishes.

I find it fascinating that Parsley belongs to the carrot family and, as such, can be treated like carrots. I never really noticed the resemblance in their leaves until I knew this fact!

I love that by simply adding this freshly chopped aromatic herb to the dishes I am serving provides my family with a plethora of vitamins and minerals. One such vitamin is K, vital for blood and bone health. It's also rich in vitamins A and C, both of which have antioxidant properties and are excellent for preventing cell damage and supporting the immune system.

Another tidbit of information that you might find interesting is that you can use both the Parsley leaves *and* roots. Interestingly, Russians have been using Parsley root for its medicinal qualities for cure-alls, poison antidotes, and to create formulas to relieve bladder and kidney stones for many years.

Now that you're more familiar with the Parsley plant, let's learn more about what keeps them happy and producing.

- **Pot Size**

Whether you grow curly (sweet and soft flavored) or flat-leaved Parsley (vibrant and strong-flavored), know that they aren't too fussy about space. So if you give your herb a small container or grow bag that is at least 6 − 8 inches (15 − 20 cm) deep, they'll appreciate the space − no questions asked! Some people, however, go wrong and overcrowd parsley plants in a container. If you want healthy plants that provide a high yield, I recommend you plant only one or two parsley plants per container.

- **Watering Frequency**

Parsley may not be fussy about space, but they are attention seekers. They love being fed and watered regularly, so be prepared to keep up your end of the nurturing and maintenance bargain. Parsley enjoys even watering but is prone to root rot, so only re-water the container by drenching it thoroughly when the soil starts to dry out. Good drainage is essential for Parsley.

- **Sunlight Requirements**

Placing your Parsley in a sunny spot for eight hours of full sun per day will keep it happy; however, if you only have a partial shade or dappled light area, that will suffice.

- **Soil Requirements**

Parsley enjoys feeding on rich, organic matter. Provide them with well-drained quality potting soil and treat them to a half-strength liquid fertilizer every month if you feel the ground isn't nutrient-rich. If you add compost or manure to every two parts of potting soil, fertilizer isn't strictly necessary.

- **Other Helpful Info**

If you're growing your Parsley outside, watch out for aphids, parsley worms, and spider mites. It's rare for these plants to get an infestation, but the culprit is usually one of those three if they do.

BASIL

From a healthy gut to a robust immune system, the benefits of Basil can be numerous. This warm, peppery, and sweet culinary herb is native to India and belongs to the Mint family. Fresh Basil leaves are one of the core ingredients used to make pesto which is a hot commodity in my home (*everybody* wants it all the time!).

You can use Basil to flavor pizzas, pasta, salads, and more. Some varieties of Basil include Sweet Basil, Lemon Basil, Italian/curly Basil, and Holy Basil (Tulsi), to name a few. Sweet Basil and Lemon Basil are amongst the most common and play a significant role in Italian and Asian cuisines, and these also happen to be my favorite types to grow.

Basil provides a decent supply of vitamin K and calcium, as well as a range of antioxidants. Adding some Basil to your diet will strengthen your digestive system and fortify your nervous system. It's interesting to note that its leaves can be a good remedy for insomnia and headaches.

Because Basil contains a good amount of eugenol, it can reduce inflammation in the digestive tract and help reduce acid in the body. In addition, Basil supports a healthy liver, detoxifies the body, cures an upset stomach, and fights various illnesses. You may have heard that growing Basil is difficult, but I guarantee you this, give Basil what they like, and they'll reward you all year long.

Here's what Basil likes:

- **Pot Size**

It's effortless to please Basil when you provide them with enough room to breathe. While Basil plants prefer fabric pots as they enjoy sufficient air circulation, these fragrant herbs will grow in almost anything, as long as it offers good drainage. It's best to provide Basil plants with a 2-gallon (9 l) container and plant them about 6 – 8 inches (15 – 20 cm) apart, which gives them sufficient growing room and also allows good circulation between the plants.

- **Watering Frequency**

Basil plants tend to be picky about their watering needs. While they do not want to get soaked, they insist on regular water, or they will quickly dry out and shrivel up. Keeping your Basil's soil moist but not soggy is essential. Do the finger test to see if it's time to re-water your plants. If the soil is becoming dry about 1 inch (2.5 cm) below the surface, it's time to re-water.

- **Sunlight Requirements**

Basil is a warm seasonal herb and adores the sun, flourishing when placed in a sunny spot. Six to eight hours of sunlight will keep them happy. However, if you feel the climate is too hot, let them enjoy a little afternoon shade. Moving your Basil indoors during winter is best for their health. I recommend waiting for two weeks after your last frost if you're wondering when it's a good time to move them outdoors again.

- **Soil Requirements**

Basil plants do not enjoy cold soil, but since you're planting them in containers, their environment will most likely be warm enough, especially if your pot is sitting in a sunny spot. Just make sure you feed your herbs with high-quality potting soil and add a slow-release organic fertilizer in spring so that they are provided with nutrients all season long.

- **Other Helpful Info**

Most people who see my Basil plants wonder how I got them to grow into vibrant bushes and not skinny tree-like plants. I achieve this by pinching the top leaves off when the plant has grown about 4 inches (10 cm) tall which helps the plant grow more side foliage and become bushier.

GREEK OREGANO

Greek Oregano is a staple in many cuisines worldwide and is used the most by Italian culinary chefs. Greek Oregano has its origin in Greece and, just like Basil, belongs to the Mint family. The Greeks associated this tasty herb with good health and good luck, and many also believe that it symbolizes joy.

Oregano, also known as Spanish Thyme or Wild Marjoram, comes from the Greek word 'joy of the mountain' and has steadily made its way around the world and into the hearts of many foodies. Oregano contains antioxidants like tryptophan, valine, lysine, arginine, and vitamins A, C, and K.

The antioxidants present in Oregano treat asthma, muscle aches, allergies, skin sores, cases of flu, and colds while boosting overall health. I personally love Oregano for its versatility. I use it in teas, stews, meat dishes, salads, and pasta. Greek Oregano tastes slightly sweet and warm, with a hint of bitterness. It's safe to say that Oregano is on the top of my container and grow bag herb list!

To grow and nurture thriving Oregano, here's what you need to know.

- **Pot Size**

Oregano can get out of control if it's not maintained, so container and grow bag gardening is a good step in the right direction for Oregano lovers. Oregano likes investigating its environment and spreads out quickly, so give them a container or grow bag that is at least 12 inches (30 cm) in diameter. If you're planting seeds instead of seedlings outdoors, start six weeks before the last frost.

- **Watering Frequency**

Oregano hates having wet feet, so take care not to overwater it. Instead, hydrate them only when the soil is dry to the touch. Water enough to moisten the top 5 inches (12 cm) of the pot. Good drainage is vital to the overall happiness of Oregano.

- **Sunlight Requirements**

Greek Oregano loves resting in a sunny spot – whether it's the windowsill of your kitchen, your balcony, or deck. Always remember that light and warmth are Oregano's best friends. So give your herbs about six to eight hours of sunlight per day.

- **Soil Requirements**

Because Oregano is a hardy plant, they don't necessarily need to be fed fertilizer or compost. They are low-maintenance and prefer light, well-drained soil. Having moderately fertile soil will keep them productive. If you want to fertilize, there is no need to do more than a very light fertilizing once a year.

- **Other Helpful Info**

Did you know Greek Oregano is an excellent companion herb? They are friendly to neighboring plants, especially tomatoes and peppers, as they act as protectors against aphids and other bugs. So, if you're growing these veggies in your garden as well, it's a good idea to position your Oregano plants directly next to and around them.

ROSEMARY

Rosemary, which translates from Latin to "dew of the sea," is also part of the Mint family. This evergreen plant is native to the rocky and dry areas of the Mediterranean region along the coast. Rosemary provides a beautiful aroma and taste to many dishes, especially roast chicken and potato dishes – trust me, these are my favorites.

For me, growing Rosemary in containers and grow bags is a must. For starters, Rosemary contains essential vitamins like A, C, and B-6 and is a good source of calcium and iron. It also has a reputation as a powerful cognitive stimulant. Rosemary improves memory quality and performance, and because of this, I am always looking for creative ways to add it to the meals I create.

To grow Rosemary successfully and enjoy a healthy yield, here's what you need to know:

- **Pot size**

Rosemary will need a container or grow bag of about 12 inches (30 cm) in diameter, giving them enough space to develop their root system properly and expand as they like to do. As is the case with most container-grown herbs, good drainage is absolutely essential.

- **Watering Frequency**

Like Oregano, Rosemary hates having wet feet. They want consistent moisture but not *constant* moisture. Rosemary plants need about 1 – 2 inches (2.5 cm – 5 cm) of water per week. If the soil feels dry at about 1 -2 inches (3 – 5 cm deep), then it's time to water your Rosemary.

- **Sunlight Requirements**

This beautiful Mediterranean plant will thrive in six hours of full sunlight. The more sunshine they're treated to, the more they will produce. Rosemary does best in the warmer months, so be prepared to provide them with a bit of extra care and protection when the colder months come around.

- **Soil Requirements**

Rosemary produces well when given a quality potting mix that includes fine pine bark. Luckily, Rosemary doesn't have a large appetite, which means that fertilizer is not a must. However, if you feel your plant's color is fading or perhaps the growth isn't quite what it used to be, you can feed it with dry fertilizer in moderation. I typically give mine a tiny amount of fertilizer in spring.

- **Other Helpful Info**

Don't let your Rosemary grow wild if you want a good yield. The plant appreciates having the top picked off before it flowers. Just before it flowers is a good time for harvesting and is when Rosemary's aroma and taste is at its peak.

THYME

One of the reasons why I love growing Thyme so much is that it has a lovely aroma. I enjoy adding dry Thyme to pizzas, roasted meat and veggies, fish dishes, and, to be honest, just about any savory dish. The origins of Thyme can be traced back to Mediterranean territories, where its use has been more than culinary.

Ancient Egyptians used Thyme in their embalming processes, and throughout history, people have used it to cure the effects of poison and relieve pain. It is now grown and enjoyed globally as a food source.

Thyme is an excellent source of both vitamin A and C, and if you're wondering where to find a source of iron, you'll find it in Thyme too! While there are many types of Thyme variants, I think you will find the following helpful in your kitchen: English, French, Lemon, and Winter Thyme. I found that these varieties grow well in containers, grow bags, and do equally well indoors and outdoors.

If you're ready to learn all you need to know about growing Thyme, let's dive right in:

- **Pot Size**

Use a 4 – 6 inch (10 – 15cm) wide pot that's 4 inches (10 cm) tall per Thyme plant, giving your Thyme the perfect environment to develop its root system and enough space to breathe.

- **Watering Frequency**

One of the reasons why Thyme is one of my favorite plants is that it is extremely low maintenance. It will go about growing happily with very little need for your attention. It does, however, enjoy 1 inch (2.5 cm) of water every 10 – 15 days. If you're watering by hand, drench the pot and only water again when the top 1 – 2 inches (2.5 cm – 5 cm) of soil is drying out. Thyme doesn't require a lot of water at all, and if it does dry out entirely, it won't have an immediate adverse effect.

- **Sunlight Requirements**

Thyme doesn't mind indirect sunlight, making it the perfect indoor plant for the kitchen window sill. That's not to say that it doesn't enjoy the sunlight. You will get the best out of your Thyme plant by providing it with six hours of full sun per day.

- **Soil Requirements**

You will probably be relieved to learn that Thyme is another herb that isn't too fussy about soil conditions. While I never recommend this, I have found that regular garden soil is enough to grow a thriving Thyme plant. Adding some potting soil, peat moss, and perlite will bring out the best in your plant.

- **Other Helpful Info**

If you want to give your Thyme plant a great growing experience, I recommend planting it in a clay container as it dries out quickly. It's essential to replant your Thyme every second season at least, as they divide and expand quickly – which means an abundance of Thyme for you!

MINT

Mint is an excellent addition to any container or grow bag garden. This fragrant herb, native to Eurasia and North America, southern Africa, and Australia, thrives in many areas. It's often grown and harvested to flavor gum and candy. Mint leaves offer small amounts of vitamin A, C, potassium, calcium, phosphorus, and magnesium.

Apart from the flavor and a mild dose of vitamins, Mint offers a wide array of other benefits too. I often use it to treat common colds in my home. It's also great for people watching their waistline as it contains digestive enzymes that can speed up metabolism and aid in weight loss.

My family thoroughly enjoys fresh Mint with lamb dishes as it makes spectacular sauces or chutneys. If you're not keen to make a sauce, use the leaves to garnish or crush them with a few squeezes of lemon and fizzy water for a zesty, summery drink.

If you've ever seen Mint growing, you probably know that it has a penchant for going wild and taking over the space around it. Container and grow bag gardening allows you to keep the Mint bush under control. If you want your Mint bush to get thicker and bushier, just keep pinching off the fragrant leaves.

Growing Mint in containers and grow bags is easy – here's what you need to know:

• Pot Size

Mint will spring up nicely in a container that is 12 inches (30 cm) in diameter and 10 – 12 inches (25 – 30 cm) deep, and I would recommend assigning only one Mint plant per container. Their roots go deep down, so if you put them in a shallow pot, you'll find these roots tend to creep out of the drainage holes and grow into the surrounding environment.

While you can plant Mint seeds, it's not the most dependable method to get going since the seeds don't always germinate. Purchasing a small Mint plant from a nursery is a far better option to get you started on your first batch. Mint won't have any particular reaction to the container you use, as long as you make sure it has suitable drainage holes.

• Watering Frequency

For your Mint plant to be fresh and lush, it needs around 1 – 2 inches (2.5 – 5 cm) of water weekly. If you aren't relying on rainfall and are watering by hand, you need to check for moisture 1 inch (2.5 cm) below the surface. If it's dry, it's time to re-water.

You'll notice that the soil tends to dry out faster if you leave it outside during hot weather, and this may leave your Mint feeling a little thirstier than usual, so increase the water supply as the seasons get warmer.

• Sunlight Requirements

Mint loves the sun. Like most herbs, Mint can tolerate the shade, but allowing it to spend five hours per day in direct sunlight will ensure it's more flavorful with a more pungent aroma.

- **Soil Requirements**

Mint enjoys spreading its roots in quality potting mix. Of course, you can go ahead and add a bit of time-release fertilizer just before you plant Mint and a little again every spring. Mint only requires a tiny amount of fertilizer as it often suppresses the flavor, which is undoubtedly something you want to avoid.

- **Other Helpful Info**

You may need to replant your Mint now and again. If you notice your Mint becoming a bit sad – it can start drying out from the center - it's time to consider repotting it. Give your Mint fresh, well-composted soil, and it should perk up again.

LEMON BALM (Melissa, Sweet Balm, Honey Plant)

If you think Lemon Balm looks like oversized Mint, you're not too far off. It is, in fact, part of the Mint family (again). Lemon Balm is native to Southern Europe but is a popular plant used in the cosmetic industry the world over.

One of the reasons you might enjoy growing Lemon Balm is that it makes a delicious tea. It has a beautiful lemony smell with just a hint of Mint. These flavors also make it perfect for seasoning chicken and fish dishes. I have also found that it makes for a great alternative to lemon when baking biscuits too.

Lemon Balm is known for its healing properties and has a reputation for reducing anxiety. Make yourself a cup of tea and feel the anxiety melt away.

I have always found it interesting that Lemon Balm is colloquially known as Melissa (which means 'bee' in Greek), Sweet

Balm, or Honey Plant. The Greeks used to plant Lemon Balm near hives to encourage honeybees to return to their hives and keep producing honey.

This sprawling plant can become quite excessive if left unattended, so it's a good thing that you will be growing it in containers and grow bags. You will find that there are many varieties from which to choose. I recommend trying the M. Officinalis variety as it grows very well anywhere. Other remarkable types that are fantastic choices for your first container and grow bag garden include Aurea, Citronella, and Compacta.

Learn the basics of Lemon Balm growing below:

- **Pot Size**

Lemon Balm will thrive in a 15 – 18 inch (38 – 46 cm) wide container that's at least 8 inches (20 cm) deep. This size container will give you a good yield, allowing you to use up a third of the leaves at a time. Lemon Balm responds well to warm weather, so I'd suggest planting seeds in a container in spring. Late spring is good, but only once all chances of frost have passed.

- **Watering Frequency**

Lemon Balm enjoys a good soak every few days, so be generous when you water them, especially in summer when you find you will need to water them daily. Drench the container until the water flows through the drainage holes. Do a finger test before watering again and only re-water when the top 1 inch (2.5 cm) of soil is starting to dry out.

- **Sunlight Requirements**

Lemon Balm doesn't mind spending time in a partly shaded area, although it does welcome at least five hours of direct sunlight a day. You can leave your container indoors if you're going to give it 14 – 16 hours of artificial light, although I must warn you that it's not the most flavorful when not exposed to direct sunlight. I find that the tastiest leaves are the young, fresh ones that have grown in direct sunlight, so find a sunny spot for your Lemon Balm and let it do its thing.

- **Soil Requirements**

Lemon Balm will produce an excellent yield when you plant them in several inches of aged compost mixed into your native soil. For the healthiest, glossiest leaves, feed your Lemon Balm with water-soluble plant food each spring.

- **Other Helpful Info**

Lemon Balm flowers are not showy, but they do drop seeds that will germinate. To prevent this from happening, add mulch around your Lemon Balm and scoop up any dropping seeds from the surface to nurture in other pots and grow bags or to discard.

I have found that herbs are some of the easiest plants to grow in containers and grow bags. They aren't nearly as fussy as fruits, veggies, and flowers, and you can add them to almost any meal and snack.

Now that you have a sound basis for herb growing let's consider a few flowers for your container garden. Let's turn to Chapter Six: *Flowers for Your Container & Grow Bag Garden* to learn how to get your container and grow bag garden bursting with color.

6

FLOWERS FOR YOUR CONTAINER & GROW BAG GARDEN

While growing veggies and herbs have always been my main focus with container and grow bag gardening, I cannot resist bringing bright splashes of color to my garden space.

Some flowers are edible, making a great addition to a salad or table décor when entertaining friends. Another side effect of having containers of colorful flowers around your veggies and herbs is that they lure insects, bees, and butterflies to your garden. As you know, these critters are responsible for pollinating your plants – this means a beautiful and productive yield for you.

I have a few favorites I would like to share with you. I chose these flowers for my own home because they are undeniably beautiful, and they are easy to grow and care for, especially for newbies to the world of gardening.

Here's a list of my favorite flowers for container and grow bag gardening. We will focus on these throughout the chapter.

- New Guinea Impatiens
- Calibrachoa
- Persian Shield
- Geranium
- Winged Begonia
- Sweet Potato Vine
- Starflower
- Petunia

Let's look at how to get these flowers blooming to the best of their ability!

NEW GUINEA IMPATIENS (Impatiens Hawkeri)

Impatiens are a real gem, in my opinion, as they are colorful and will grow like wildfire if you give them a suitable environment. These beauties are native to Papua New Guinea and are widespread throughout the Northern Hemisphere and the tropics. You may find it interesting that North America Impatiens are used as herbal remedies to treat insect bites, bee stings, and stinging nettle rashes. We have put them to good use in my home when we've had the occasional insect bite or bee sting.

New Guinea Impatiens (Impatiens Hawkeri) are known by many names in North America: Touch-Me-Not, Jewelweed, Snapweed (my favorite name for them, by the way), Patience, and of course Impatiens.

I have found that New Guinea Impatiens take to containers and grow bags easily, which is undoubtedly good news for you. They come in various colors, including coral, scarlet, pink, salmon, violet, cherry red, to name the most common. Having a mix of each variant will invite beautiful butterflies to your garden.

Here's what you need to know about the lifestyle Impatiens enjoy:

- **Pot Size**

I typically choose containers and hanging baskets for my Impatiens, and I recommend you do the same. Their size varies from 8 – 48 inches (20 cm – 1 meter) tall and 6 – 36 inches (15 cm – nearly a meter) wide. They need a fair amount of space. To start, look for a pot that's about 14 – 16 inches (35 – 40c m) with enough drainage holes. New Guinea Impatiens will explore their environment and fill the space quickly, so it's crucial to increase the size of the next pot when it has outgrown the current pot. If you don't, you might find your Impatiens becoming spindly and might even die.

- **Watering Frequency**

I like to refer to my Impatiens as my water guzzlers – they *adore* water, so give them an early-morning drench. You will need to water them twice a day in summer. They aren't, however, overly sensitive to being forgotten about. If you miss a few watering sessions, they will do just fine. They may droop a bit and look damaged, but give them a drink of water, and voila, they bounce back quickly! It's best not to test out this "feature" too often though, as it still stresses the plant.

- **Sunlight Requirements**

I love New Guinea Impatiens because they can tolerate full sun, unlike other impatiens, which are shade-lovers. However, I should caution you; just because your Impatiens can endure full sun doesn't mean they should be left in the sun all day. Impatiens still enjoy light shade. Morning sun and afternoon shade are best for their health. Six to eight hours of direct sunlight keep them happy, so aim for that.

- **Soil Requirements**

Apart from being water guzzlers, your gems have good appetites too! New Guinea Impatiens feed on rich, well-drained soil. Therefore, use high-quality professionally prepared potting soil, especially ones that contain vermiculite and high perlite. Before planting, add a dry, slow-release fertilizer (20 – 20 – 20 formula) as this will ensure your flowers get their nutrients when they need it the most. Aim to fertilize your impatiens three times a year.

- **Other Helpful Info**

While New Guinea Impatiens do well if they are just left to grow, they prefer if you give them a little attention when planted in a pot. Here's what you do: pick them up and give them a gentle shake, ridding them of the old blossoms. Then, to keep them in shape and guide their growth, occasionally trim them to allow more flowering.

CALIBRACHOA (Million Bells, Trailing-Petunia)

Calibrachoa's first registered name is 'Million Bells' and is also called the Trailing-Petunia. Its name comes from the fact that it contains hundreds of tiny bell-like flowers that look like mini Petunias.

Calibrachoa is a tender perennial plant producing mounds of colorful foliage spanning the rainbow and finds its origin in South America – mostly Chile, Peru, and southern Brazil. Growing these bells is super easy, and they are prolific bloomers right from spring until the first frosts of winter.

The sheer variety of these flowers (and I have several of them) is exquisite. I am always gobsmacked when they are in full bloom. It's fun choosing the best varieties for you. You will find that some have a dark and mysterious eye in the center of the flower while others have a bright sunny eye. Whether you choose a striped bloom, a yellow star pattern that radiates from the center of the flower, or a single or double flower, you really can't go wrong. I recommend hanging a basket of these flowers outside your kitchen window if you live in an area where hummingbirds are present. It will attract them, and you will get to admire these beautiful birds up close.

Let's find out what keeps these pretty little bells in colorful bloom.

- **Pot Size**

Because calibrachoa has a trailing nature, they seem to thrive in hanging baskets. They grow to about 6 – 10 inches (15 – 25 cm) tall and 18 – 24 inches (46 – 61 cm) wide. If you're choosing a pot, one single plant will cover it entirely with billowing flowers making them ornamental in appearance. I just can't get over how stunning they look.

These flowers aren't too picky about their living conditions, so get a container or grow bag that offers sufficient drainage. It needs to be about 12 inches (30 cm) deep and wide. You will find that the bells like the company of other bells – it's nice to huddle three plants together in a container shaped like a triangle as this will allow them to make a pretty circle as they grow.

- **Watering Frequency**

Unlike the Impatiens we discussed earlier, these bells aren't water guzzlers. They do, however, need a moist environment to thrive. Ensure you hydrate them every week during their growing season by lightly watering the container. Let the soil start to dry out before you water it again. If you're in a much warmer climate, you can water them every day, but don't soak them, though, just aim to keep them moist.

- **Sunlight Requirements**

Calibrachoa are sun lovers, and while they don't mind the shade, they prefer the sun a lot more. The more sunlight you give them, the more flowers they will produce. Six hours of sun daily should be the minimum, but up to eight hours is ideal.

- **Soil Requirements**

These flowers aren't particularly demanding when it comes to nutrition, but I find feeding them regularly makes them strong and productive. To keep them happy, they'll need a good quality potting mix and regular fertilization. It's good to feed them a water-soluble fertilizer every two weeks. However, I prefer a slow-release granular fertilizer because it ensures my flowers get a dose of nutrients when needed, and I don't have to fertilize quite so often (only every couple of months).

- **Other Helpful Info**

If you would like to plant bells as a seed, the seed series named 'Kabloom' is your best choice. You will see there's a palate of colors to choose from, including pink, purple, peach, blue, violet, and white. All other calibrachoas grow from cuttings.

If planting as seedlings, they need about 8 – 10 weeks to grow to maturity. Try to sow seeds about eight weeks before the last frost. You can start by planting them indoors. Instead of covering the seedling with soil, press the seeds lightly into the potting soil surface. The seedlings like plenty of light, so try to keep them in a spot where they will receive a full day's sunlight. You should notice them sprouting in 10 – 14 days!

PERSIAN SHIELD (Strobilanthes Dyerianus)

Persian Shields are beautiful, and I like to think of their burst of color being a beautiful armor around our deck! What's great about this particular flower is that it lasts all year long.

The Persian Shield gets its name from the appearance of its armor-like shield leaves. Even though its name implies that it originates from Persia, it doesn't. Persian Shield is native to Myanmar (Burma), south of Asia. This drop-dead gorgeous foliage boasts a flashy, purple iridescence with an almost silver metallic sheen. Persian Shields have become one of the more popular houseplants due to their ability to bloom during winter and are perfect for container and grow bag gardening.

Scientists believe that the Persian Shield's purple foliage acts like a 'sunscreen,' protecting the plant's cells from extreme light, thereby helping them retain their vibrant color year-round.

Here are all the necessary details you need to introduce this pretty armor-like plant to your container and grow bag garden.

- **Pot Size**

Persian Shields grow to a whopping 18 – 36 inches (45 – 91 cm) tall and wide! You need to select a container that gives it enough room to develop and grow strong roots. You can start with a pot size that's 12 inches (30 cm) deep and wide. When your shrub outgrows this, increase the pot size by 1 to 2 inches (2.5 – 5 cm) each time.

- **Watering Frequency**

I wouldn't say Persian Shields are thirsty plants. However, they do need you to water them thoroughly and evenly once or twice a week. Remember, the less you hydrate them, the more shade they will need. If left unwatered, they will start to droop and look a little lifeless. To solve this, give them a drink, and they bounce right back up. When watering Persian Shields, soak the container or grow bag and then do a finger test before you water again. They need re-watering when the top 3 inches (7.5 cm) of soil are starting to dry out.

- **Sunlight Requirements**

Persian Shields do very well in both full sun and full shade. I have found that giving them around six hours of sunlight a day brings out their true beauty. It's almost as if their colors are beaming at us from the deck. Placing Persian Shields in partial shade will allow them to pick up light and reflect it off their leaves, providing a shimmery effect. If esthetics are important to you – this is definitely the flower choice for your container and grow bag garden.

- **Soil Requirements**

Persian Shields can tolerate slightly acidic soil. If your soil is moist and rich, then add well-balanced liquid fertilizer every two weeks in its growing season. Flower fertilizer from your local garden center will do just fine as it encourages strong root development. Once fall approaches, slow down the feeding schedule to monthly and resume bi-weekly feeding at the beginning of spring.

- **Other Helpful Info**

The best time to grow these Persian Shields is during fall. However, make sure you take your flowers in when winter approaches as they don't flower in the cold. If they're inside during the colder months, they may reward you with tiny violet flowers.

GERANIUM (Pelargonium Hybrids)

Remember I said *some* flowers are edible? Well, Geraniums are one of those flowers. My favorite variants are the Pelargonium Hybrids, so keep an eye out for those. These beauties are native to South Africa and grow in the Cape of Good Hope. The plants eventually made their way to Europe, where they remain a popular plant today.

Geraniums are cultivated all around the world. Both the aromatic foliage and the Geranium flower are edible. If we have guests coming over, we love to dress up our salads and desserts with them.

Geraniums are classified into two main groups:

1. Annual Geraniums (Pelargonium types) – these flowers last for a year and include scented and ivy, fancy-leaf, zonal, and regal (Martha Washington) types.
2. Perennial Geraniums (Geranium types) – these flowers return season after season and display eye-catching leaves with flowers.

I grow the annual geraniums because they thrive best in container and grow bag gardens. Here are a few things you will need to learn about these fragrant, colorful plants to keep them happy.

- **Pot Size**

I advise you to plant scented Pelargonium for its wide range of culinary use. Because this culinary flower can grow anywhere from 4 – 48 inches (10 cm – 1.2 meters) tall and 6 – 36 inches (15 – 91 cm) wide, you'll want to give them enough room to grow and explore. Annual geranium types prefer a pot size of at least 10 inches (25 cm) in diameter. They get along quite nicely with other varieties of Geraniums, but if you're planning on adding multiple plants, make sure you give them a little space to expand. Set them about 8 – 12 inches (20 – 30 cm) apart.

If you want to pot perennial geraniums, you will need to give them slightly more room - a container that's 12 inches (30 cm) will do just fine. Of course, make sure the containers you're using have excellent drainage as they don't enjoy wet feet.

- **Watering Frequency**

Annual Geraniums don't have high water demands. Water them once a week or only when the soil's top 1 inch (2.5 cm) is dry. Do a finger test before watering. To retain a bit of moisture, you can add a layer of mulch to the top surface of the soil.

- **Sunlight Requirements**

Annual Geraniums do best with six to eight hours of full sun, except the Ivy Geranium variant, which prefers light shade.

- **Soil Requirements**

Annual Geraniums have a few requirements. They flourish in well-drained potting soil, which needs equal amounts of soil, peat, and perlite. In addition, fertilizing is usually necessary, so feed them with a water-soluble houseplant fertilizer every month or so throughout their developing season.

WINGED BEGONIA

Winged Begonias are easily recognizable because of their wing-shaped leaves and are low-maintenance plants. Their beautiful red, pink, or white flowers will cheer you up for three seasons of the year.

There are two types of Winged Begonias - Angel Wings and Dragon Wings. They are both perfect for containers and grow bags, and you will find they make stunning table arrangements. Although people often refer to both variants interchangeably, their foliage and growth habits set them apart. We can distinguish Angel Wing Begonias by serrated, obliquely-shaped leaves, and these leaves can grow to be 5 – 6 inches (13 – 15 cm). The leaves are usually spotted or frosted.

Interestingly, people have crossed the Angel Wing and Wax Leaf Begonia to develop the Dragon Wing Begonia. The Dragon Wings' stems arch gracefully, and their leaves are glossy green and grow to around 2 – 5 inches (5 – 13 cm) long. Begonias originated from the tropics, so when you allow them to grow in a humid area with good air circulation and diffused light, they'll reward you with glossy leaves and attractive flowers.

Here's what you need to know about growing Winged Begonias in containers and grow bags:

- **Pot Size**

A 12 – 18 inch (30 – 45 cm) tall pot is sufficient for Winged Begonias. I also find that the Dragon Winged Begonias look exquisite in hanging baskets. Their stems and blooms find their way over the basket, creating a gorgeous display. Strangely enough, Winged Begonias enjoy being pot-bound, so a smaller pot size will make them happy.

- **Watering Frequency**

Angel and Dragon Winged Begonias are semi-hardy – they store moisture in their stems. Water the container or grow bag thoroughly and then only water again when the first 1 – 2 inches (2.5 – 5cm) of soil is dry. You can water them every three days during the summer as they tend to increase their water consumption during hotter months. They don't like wet feet, so ensure that they're never sitting in a saucer of water or are watered every day.

- **Sunlight Requirements**

Winged Begonias are shade-lovers. They prefer filtered light, so they'll be happy if you leave them under trees or on a patio. They can tolerate the morning sun, but they'll produce more vibrant colors in the shade.

- **Soil Requirements**

An organic soil that drains well will do wonders for your Winged Begonias. To keep them blooming, fertilize with half-strength fertilizer once every two months. They'll enjoy a water-soluble fertilizer such as fish emulsion.

- **Other Helpful Info**

Winged Begonias thrive best in cold, shady areas but don't like a lot of rain. It's best to move them to a sheltered location when the weather turns.

SWEET POTATO VINE

Sweet Potato Vines, which are native to tropical America, are one of my favorites as they cascade almost poetically around the containers and grow bags they are in. The leaves of the Potato Vine are huge and provide a lush and lovely appeal to any space where they are included.

The plant is available in lively greens, rich deep purples, and golden-orange colors.

I like to combine different varieties in containers and grow bags to create an appealing effect. The Margarita is a gold color that turns light green in the shade. It's a good choice for border edging or a hanging basket.

The heart-shaped Sweet Caroline Sweetheart Lime is a compact variety that pairs well with mounding Petunias in a container. The Sweet Caroline Jet Black is such a deep purple, you'll think it's black. A similar color but narrow leaves is the

Sweet Caroline Raven which is also excellent in a container. The striking contrast when paired with foliage or flowering plants makes this variety a must-have.

Finally, Sweet Caroline Bewitched Green with Envy is a variety I have to mention. This one is a heat-lover and looks gorgeous when paired with bright and cheery Calibrachoa or Petunias.

Here's how to give your Sweet Potato Vines the best life in containers and grow bags.

- **Pot Size**

Sweet Potato Vines will happily grow in a 4 – 12 inch (10 – 30 cm) tall pot. Their edible tubers will be content to make their way down the container.

- **Watering Frequency**

Moderate moisture is the key to get your Sweet Potato Vines sprawling. Drench the container or grow bag and only water again when the soil is starting to dry out 1 inch (2.5 cm) from the surface. Give them time to dry out nicely as they don't like overwatering.

- **Sunlight Requirements**

While they can take some shade, Sweet Potato Vines will reward you with intense color if you give them six hours of full sunlight each day. They will grow just as well in the shade, but you can expect their colors to be far less intense.

- **Soil Requirements**

Container vines find high-quality, all-purpose potting soil appealing. If you want them to gain growing momentum, apply a slow-release fertilizer at the time of planting. After that, you can treat your vines to water-soluble fertilizer once a month.

- **Other Helpful Info**

Sweet Potato Vines can grow expansively. They'll make the most of their space, especially when you provide them with their preferred growing conditions. As they spread quite prolifically, they can quickly outgrow their area and containers, so prune and shape them as needed. Lastly, be sure to keep your leaves out of reach of pets as they can be toxic, especially to dogs.

STARFLOWER (Egyptian Stars)

If large clusters of tiny-shaped stars pique your interest, then you'll want the charming Starflower growing in your container and grow bag garden. The Starflower is a fast-growing herbaceous shrub, and when you take good care of it, you'll have myriads of butterflies making their way to it and the rest of your garden.

Native to Yemen and East Africa, the Starflower (the Pentas Lanceolata variety) is commonly known as "Egyptian Stars". What I love about these flowers is that they bloom all year round. In addition to this, they're evergreen plants that come in a variety of colors, including tones of red, purple, white, lavender, and pink.

Below is everything you need to know about growing starflowers in containers and grow bags.

- **Pot Size**

While Starflowers thrive in containers and grow bags, they like their space. A 10 – 24 inch (25 – 61 cm) container will work well for Starflowers.

- **Watering Frequency**

You can go ahead and water Starflowers when the first inch of soil is dry and never before. They like their moisture about the same as that of a wrung-out sponge. Regular irrigation keeps them healthy, but they can tolerate dry conditions.

- **Sunlight Requirements**

Starflowers will proliferate in full sun to part shade. If you give them a minimum of three hours of direct sunlight per day, they'll bloom perfectly. If you don't give them three hours at least, they'll stretch out and become leggy. If you're planning to keep them indoors, you should know they prefer a warm room with bright light and no drafts. I find that they do fine outdoors in the spring once temperatures reach 65 degrees Fahrenheit (18 degrees Celsius).

- **Soil Requirements**

When providing soil for your Starflowers, know they thrive in mildly acidic soil (a pH range of about 6 is ideal). If your soil is on the alkaline side, I'd recommend adding leaf mold to increase the acidity of your soil. During periods of active growth, your Starflowers will appreciate well-balanced, time-release flower fertilizer at least once every three months.

- **Other Helpful Info**

By pinching off the stem ends, you force a more compact plant with more blooms. By encouraging more blooms, you attract more butterflies, and you may see a hummingbird too!

PETUNIA

I like to think of Petunias as little show-offs. Native to South America, these plants come in an abundance of colors and range from being spotted to speckled. Deep crimson and violet flecked ones are spectacular, and the solid colors with white edgings look smart. I must admit I have tried many different variants.

The flowers themselves are fascinating, some producing ruffled and fringed petals, and others have smooth edges. There's also a range of sizes from which to choose. Some are as big as the palm of your hand, while others are cute and petite. When selecting the best variety for your container, opt for special trailing Petunias as these perform dramatically in containers. However, with the proper care, any Petunia will thrive in containers and grow bags.

Petunias are pretty easy to please – here's what you need to know about growing them in containers and grow bags.

- **Pot Size**

A 12 inch (30 cm) container or grow bag is a decent size to house your Petunias. A hanging basket will also encase them well, allowing them to drape over the edge. Petunias love to produce new blooms significantly when you cut them back. For this reason, limiting yourself to three plants per 12 inch pot is best.

- **Watering Frequency**

Petunias don't like being drenched – they prefer to sip water. They're happier when you water their soil directly and avoid wetting the foliage. Carefully lift the flowers to avoid getting them wet. Water them once a week, allowing the water to soak through to the roots. Petunias are dry, hardy plants, so you'll want to ensure that your container has good drainage.

- **Sunlight Requirements**

If there's any flower that loves to soak the sun, it's the Petunia. Six hours of direct sunlight brings them to life. However, if you can get them positioned nicely to sunbathe for eight hours a day, they will absolutely thrive.

- **Soil Requirements**

A free-draining soilless potting mix works best for potted Petunias. Fortify your soil with a slow-release fertilizer at least once a month.

- **Other Helpful Info**

Take care of the Petunias' root system as it is a weak system and often causes them to die. You want them to develop sturdy roots that are well-rooted in the pot. Water them deeply as shallow watering encourages shallow roots.

7

TROUBLESHOOTING COMMON CONTAINER GARDEN PROBLEMS

Over the past 5 years, as an avid container and grow bag gardener, I have made plenty of mistakes along the way. While I believe making mistakes is a great learning curve for anyone, especially me, I also think that it's great to learn from other's mistakes. I have pieced together some of the common container gardening mistakes and problems you may encounter along the way and how to overcome/avoid them. I hope that this helps you enjoy the most rewarding container and grow bag gardening experience possible.

MOVING A HEAVY CONTAINER

If you're like me and have many potted plants, you may need to move them around to protect them from harsh weather conditions or to improve the esthetics of your home. However, in saying this, moving potted plants often puts them at risk.

Your plants could suffer from low heat, water, and light, ultimately causing severe damage. In addition, while moving heavier containers around, you could injure yourself. Here are a few things you may want to consider when moving containers – especially weighty ones:

- **Be aware of the risks**

One of the risks of moving containers around is disrupting the soil layers in the container or grow bag. When you move your plant to a different environment, whether indoors to outdoors or sun to shade, you're ultimately changing the moisture, wind, and temperature of its living conditions. If you're going to move your potted plant, make sure that you're not putting it in a tricky spot, literally and figuratively.

- **Plan ahead**

Failing to plan is planning to fail, as the saying goes. Before filling and planting in a sizeable container, know where the final location of the plant will be. Place the empty container in its final position, then begin filling and planting in the container or grow bag. Suppose your potted plants are outdoors, and bringing them indoors during winter is a requirement; you should rather invest in caddies on wheels, a trundler (small frame on casters), or something similar. Proper handling will prevent physical strain on your body, avoiding impending injury and muscle spasms.

- **Choose new locations carefully**

Remember, don't move plants in heavy containers and grow bags unless it's necessary. I cannot stress this enough. Prepare your plant's environment, especially if it's a hefty or a tall/wide plant. The new environment needs to be comfortable for your container plant, meaning the location you choose needs to provide your plant with the required aeration and light. Also, make sure that you can access the plant easily from all sides as this will help you when it's time to water, inspect the plant for diseases and pests, or harvest your fruit, veggies, and foliage.

PURCHASING PLANTS THAT DON'T GO WELL TOGETHER

As with traditional gardens, a beautiful container or grow bag garden begins with the perfect blend of plants. Whether you're creating a combination vegetable planter or a flower container garden, you must purchase compatible plants. If you select incompatible plants, this will lead to the aggressive plants stealing the nutrition of your more passive plants.

Even though the initial glance at your garden may look relaxed and tranquil, your plants may be fighting a vicious battle against each other. When it comes to building a container or grow bag garden full of different colorful flowers and plants, you should consider some essential things.

- **Choose plants for more than just esthetics**

When selecting plants, keep in mind that it has to be about more than just color schemes and esthetic appeal. You need to establish whether or not your plants are compatible with each other, especially if they share a container or space. I don't mean you should solely choose plants with similar needs (sunlight, soil, and water requirements), even though this is important. Instead, I'm talking about researching which types of plants to pair up because they should have similar behaviors and attitudes.

Plants that don't get along will fight for the resources they need to survive, such as soil nutrients, sunlight, and water. Therefore, pair plants with similar strengths and then monitor their behavior. Please note that not all plants grow at the same rate, no matter how healthy they are. Choose varieties with similar growth rates where one plant will not dominate the others in the container or in their separate containers, such as competing for sunlight.

- **Identify and research plant behavior**

There are 3 types of container plants: aggressive plants, passive (tolerant) plants, and assertive (bold) plants.

Aggressive plants are more often than not annuals because you raise them to grow fast and strong for a short season. Assertive (bold) plants are mostly perennials or edibles (vegetables and herbs). Passive plants are slow-growing plants (common houseplants). If you start pairing aggressive plants and passive (tolerant) plants together, you'll create a war, although it is a silent one.

Assertive plants may be a bit more flexible. Again, do some research before going to the nursery to purchase an array of plants for your container garden. Get some information from a garden center, and read plant instructions carefully. All these things matter if you want your container garden to flourish.

UNDERFEEDING

Whatever you planted in containers, whether herbs, fruit, and veggies, or flowers, they are all restricted to the nutrients contained in the potting soil you provide for them.

The nutrients get used up fairly quickly, which isn't surprising if you reuse the same soil mix every season, and this is why fertilizer is such a vital ingredient to sustain healthy plants. Unfortunately, not many people know that fertilizer is essential, not optional, to their plants' lives.

The only way your plants can produce flowers or a good crop yield is if they're fed nutrients (fertilizer) regularly, especially during their growing season. Without this, your plants remain stunted in their growth and never produce an abundant harvest of crops.

- **Select quality potting mix**

The majority of potting mixes comprise a couple of nutrients that plants need to stay healthy. These nutrients get absorbed quickly through the plant's root system and are filtered out of the container every time they get watered. So, to keep your potted plants well-fed, you need to provide organic matter and supplemental food.

In addition, try and refresh your soil at the beginning of the next season by mixing in fresh potting soil or mixing compost. By doing this, you're giving your potted plants an excellent start for a fruitful garden season ahead. Remember that no single potting mix is perfect for all container plants. Visit a garden center or do some internet research regarding the ideal potting mix to grow your particular plants.

- **The value of fertilizing**

You'll notice that most commercial potting mixes that are graded 'high-quality' have a small amount of fertilizer included to give freshly potted plants a boost of nutrients, thus kick-starting their growth. However, these nutrients only last a few weeks. They don't cover the full range of nutritional elements needed in the long run, which is why I highly recommend a regular fertilizer regime.

There are different kinds of fertilizer, like slow-release ones, water-soluble ones, granular ones, and more. Each plant species needs a different type of fertilizer. In addition, certain plants need "feeding," while some essentially get poisoned or damaged if you feed them too often or feed them the wrong food.

Find out the best type of fertilizer for your plants, and then fertilize your container and grow bag garden regularly if you want your plants to stay healthy, productive, and well-nourished.

OVERWATERING

While excessive watering can cause severe damage to your plants and allow them to drown unintentionally, overwatering is not always giving your plant too much water.

If you water your plant too often or have a container or grow bag that doesn't drain properly, you could end up overwatering your plant. Perhaps your plant is growing in a container that holds onto the water without sufficient air.

Whatever the case may be, watering is an art form, which means it will take you some time to get to know your plants and how often they want you to water them. In addition, of course, there are many factors you need to consider, such as the plant's container size, wind, and sun exposure. Therefore, you must treat each plant individually.

- **Ensure proper drainage**

Overwatering your plants shows up in different ways. Some common signs of overwatered plants include yellowing leaves, soft stems, leaves turning brown around the edges, or signs of mold.

Any container you plan to use needs to have drainage holes for excess water to escape. If water is left standing at the bottom of the container without being adequately drained, you risk root rot and other plant diseases. Never use dirt you recently dug up from your garden and add it to your container as garden soil is dense and doesn't drain well. Instead, invest in quality potting soil. Carefully read and follow the instructions for the soil requirements for your plant.

Don't allow your container or grow bag to sit in stagnant water, or the soil will be too wet, and your plants will die due to lack of oxygen.

Also, never water your plants at night – unless they have already wilted. Watering plants at night usually breeds diseases because the soil stays too moist throughout the night. If your pot does not have proper drainage holes, then try and create additional space around the roots so that air can flow in and provide the plant with oxygen.

Finally, water when the soil is dry to the touch, but never let it get too dry. In saying this, continuously monitor the behavior of your plant rather than just relying on outside help or research.

WEAK POT-TO-PLANT RATIO

Choosing the number of crops for the size of the pot you have is not a one-size-fits-all ratio. You need to determine the number of plants you allow in a single pot beforehand and whether or not you need to transfer one or all of them to bigger pots in the future. Sometimes, the same plant may require 3 – 4 containers and not one large one; check first before planting.

Here is some valuable information I can share with you.

- **Signs your containers are overcrowded**

Because plants grown in a container or grow bag have limited space, they can become overcrowded. Here are signs that indicate you've planted too many plants in the pot:

1. Stunted plants: If your plant is not growing actively during its growth period, it's likely because the root system is restricted with no room to expand. You'll have to be extra careful when reducing the number of plants in a container as root systems may have become intertwined, and you'll have to ease the roots apart before replanting the excess crops in another pot.

2. Wilting: When you overcrowd a container, plants may wilt. When you notice your plants' leaves deteriorating frequently, yet they revive once watered, it means their roots are not getting enough water, and you needed a bigger pot for your plant. If your plant wilts and doesn't revive after watering, it's one of two causes: pests or diseases have damaged the roots, and you will have to check the root systems, or maybe the pot is too big. Replant in a smaller pot.

3. Escaping: A definite sign that your pot is overcrowded is when you see the plant's root system creeping from the drainage holes. Transfer your plant to a bigger pot.

- **Double potting**

When pots become overcrowded, plants are less likely to grow. Initially, you think the container is acceptable because the plants are still in baby stages, and you intend to get a bigger pot later. Take note of plants with rapid growth.

My advice is to get the larger container now rather than later. The reason is that we tend to forget, and by the time we realize it, it's too late.

The best thing to do is purchase a container that is one size larger in diameter. For vigorously growing plants, purchase an additional container that is two sizes larger. Place the smaller container in the larger one and fill it with mulch. This technique is known as double potting and is one of the best tricks of the trade. Repotting is best done in early spring before plants start actively growing.

- **Plant size proportions**

Consider the proportion of the pot to the size of the plant. Some plants cannot grow when there is insufficient space or even, in some cases, too much room for them to grow. Your container size must match the plants' growth; otherwise, you restrict the roots, leading to decreased plant growth. When the container size is out of proportion, it can also reduce the number of flowers and fruits.

When filling a container with different varieties, place your tallest plant in the center if you're leaving it in an open space or the back of the pot if you're leaving it against a wall. Place a sprawling vine over the edge. Consider using Potato Vines for the borders of your containers and grow bags.

BUYING SICK OR WEAK PLANTS

Container plant care starts before you purchase your plant. You want to start your container gardening off properly by choosing healthy, attractive, and high-quality plants.

Here is some expert advice in selecting the best plants from your local nursery or big box stores since their prices are enticing and sometimes it's hard to resist.

- **Choose your local nursery**

I wouldn't trust buying plants online as you can never guarantee quality. The best place to start is your local nursery. The reason being you can thoroughly inspect plants and get help from knowledgeable staff. People usually take excellent care of plants at local nurseries.

However, that doesn't mean you can pick any plant that looks great and expect it to thrive. It would be best if you were a bit cautious. Here's how you should examine a plant before bringing it home:

- Lift the plant and inspect it from all sides. Check that the plant is whole and that there are no empty areas or dying sides - plant growth must be sturdy, not spindly.
- Check the potting mix for weeds, and be sure to check the foliage. There should be no holes, and the color should not be faded or washed out. Also, inspect the underside of leaves to check for insects and signs of disease.
- Sometimes houseplants are sprayed with leaf shines to make them more attractive. Leaf shines, however, contain unnatural polish that clogs plants' stomates, and you should avoid them.
- Finally, check the roots. If at all possible, gently slide the plant out of its container. A healthy plant root system consists of white or tan roots growing toward the bottom or sides. Plants that have roots horizontally circling inside the container indicate the plant is root-bound, and you will stunt its growth if you take it home. So, avoid these plants.

- **Grocery store plants**

Your local grocery stores sell plants that may entice you. Be cautious as not all grocery stores can care for their plants. However, if you're applying the tips above and there's a good indication of a healthy plant, go ahead and consider purchasing.

- **Well-cared-for plants**

Sometimes it may be enticing to get cuttings from friends and family members. Their plants, however, may have adapted to their environment for years, and when you bring them home, plants may be stressed and can even die within a day.

There's the added worry you could bring diseases and pests along with cuttings. The best place to get well-cared-for plants is your local nursery, and don't be shy to ask the knowledgeable staff for advice as they have a wealth of information to help you.

- **Dealing with weak, sick plants**

You need to keep a record of where you're getting specific plants from since buying weak and sick plants can lead to infected plants, and some plants may never yield fruit at all. Here's how to deal with unhealthy plants:

- If you notice your plant has tiny yellow spots that start to grow and turn tan or dark brown in the center, then avoid wetting the foliage and remove the diseased leaves with scissors. Clean the scissors with disinfectant and wipe with a clean cloth to avoid spreading the disease.
- If plants show little to no growth and start turning yellow and show dying foliage, you must examine the roots. If small roots are affected, wash the old soil from the roots, cut diseased parts out with sterile pruners and leave only the healthy roots. Then replant in a clean pot and avoid overwatering. Root diseases spread quickly, and small infected parts will infect most of the root system within a few days, so discard a diseased plant as it is unlikely to recover.
- If spots are light green or translucent, your plant may be experiencing a bacterial foliar disease. These spots happen when your plant cannot tolerate the humidity level, it's possibly overcrowded, and/or you've wet the foliage. You should either replant your crop for space needs, move it to an area with better conditions, and avoid watering the leaves.

- Sooty mold is a black-grey mold found on leaves produced by honeydew secreting insects. When the mold is too thick, it stops the leaf's photosynthetic process. It's not detrimental to your plants but wipe the leaves with a sponge and warm water to clean them and manage the honeydew excreting insects.

- **Big box stores**

We know big box stores offer competitive pricing, so the best thing to do is find out the delivery day of new plants by asking an employee which day of the week new stock arrives and buy the plants on or close to the day they arrive.

FAILURE TO PRUNE PLANTS

Planting is only the groundwork, but maintenance is the heart of gardening. Pruning a plant is one of the best practices that a container gardener should use. Failure to prune may hinder your plants' full potential, whether you're pinching with your fingers or using a pair of shears. Here's how to prune:

- **Remove overgrowth**

Pinching fall-blooming perennial flowers early in the season will prevent your plants from becoming tall and floppy. When you prune, you restore a plant's initial growth habit, so don't be afraid to thin out the overgrowth. You can use a good pair of garden pruners to make a clean cut, especially if your plants are in a larger container and you need to make many cuts. Your fingers will do a better job in some cases. Cut stems just before they attach to a thicker branch.

- **Remove the spindly legs and dead leaves**

To protect a plant's health, you must remove dead, damaged, and diseased leaves, stems, and flowers as soon as possible. Leggy plants that are tall, thin, and weak can become stronger with a bit of pruning. When you cut back, you force new growth, even if the new development is later than anticipated.

- **Healthy haircuts**

Pruning a plant is like giving it a good haircut. Don't be afraid to cut a lot. If you are scared, I'd recommend cutting two-thirds of half the plant. After a couple of weeks, when the new plant has grown back, you can cut two-thirds of the other half.

SETTING UNREALISTIC EXPECTATIONS

Creating a container garden will perform wonders for your home, whether you're planting beautiful flowers to enjoy a burst of color in the summer or whether you know the nutritional value of a veggie grow-bag garden. However, many people see all the benefits and begin to set unrealistic expectations for their container gardens. Below are a few tips for curbing unrealistic expectations.

- **Time**

How much time are you willing to spend on your plants? Most people dedicate themselves to their plants' needs within the first few weeks, but after that, their enthusiasm begins to dwindle. Some people feel they have more important tasks that take priority and aren't in tune with the needs of their plants.

Some plants don't like missing a watering schedule, and if you're planning a summer vacation trip, will someone take care of your plants? These are essential things all newbie gardeners should consider. The best thing is to create reminders to tell yourself which months certain plants need relocation or fertilization and when to water them. It's easy to remember if you're planting herb pots in your kitchen as you'll likely see them often, but do consider containers that may not always be in sight.

- **Have reasonable expectations**

Remember that container and grow bag gardening can be a trial-and-error process. You may like the intended esthetics of your garden, but sometimes what you expect and what you get can be two different things. It's good to experiment with ideas, but remember to leave room for learning.

- **Horticultural practicality**

People use different techniques and employ different standards when caring for a garden. Don't be afraid to experiment with a variety of colors, but also consider horticultural practicality. Consider the plant you want to grow, the conditions it prefers, and whether or not your available space can provide all it needs.

For instance, if you are keen to grow a sun-loving plant but have no sunshine on your balcony or small garden space, don't put the plant through the trauma of "seeing if it will grow." Unfortunately, plants have their needs, and if you can't provide them with what they need, they will wither and die.

Now that you're thinking along the lines of caring for your container and grow bag plants, I would like to take things up a level. So let's page over to Chapter Eight: *Tips & Tricks for a Beautiful Container & Grow Bag Garden.*

8

TIPS AND TRICKS FOR A BEAUTIFUL CONTAINER GARDEN

There is more to a thriving container and grow bag garden than simply potting plants and letting them grow. Planning a beautiful garden space, regardless of how small it might be, will ensure your container and grow bag garden isn't just neat and esthetically appealing but gives you the best possible yield too.

Below are a few tips and tricks I have learned along the way. I hope these come in handy when planning, setting up, and caring for your container and grow bag garden.

PLANT WITH A PLAN

Like every other hobby, container gardening requires careful thought by the newbie gardener. Even though garden centers and nurseries globally have an array of healthy, beautiful-looking plants, keeping them flourishing and looking good throughout the seasons is tricky.

Put some forethought into the process before you get started. Draw up a rough sketch of how you want to set things up and try to make a list of all the things you will need. The more exhaustive your list is, the better. In addition, before heading to a garden center or nursery to purchase a lovely selection of pots and containers/grow bags; keep the following in mind:

- **Pots matter**

Choosing the right size pots for your plants is the first step to creating a successful container and grow bag garden. Here are a few factors that you will need to consider before purchasing pots.

- Pot type:

There are various pot styles and materials from which to choose, but no matter what pot you select, make sure it has enough drainage holes so that excess water can drain out quickly. Not having drainage holes will lead to root rot, stunted growth, plant suffocation, and eventually death. Choose a pot with an excellent drainage system that allows aeration for your container plants because it's difficult for them to access oxygen in a container, unlike plants that you place in the ground.

- Undersized pots:

Compact containers and grow bags that are not large enough to accommodate your selection of plants will crowd the roots, leading to a scarcity of oxygen, water, and nutrients.

- Oversized pots:

If your containers are too big for your plants, the soil will be too moist, cut off the plants' oxygen, and drown their roots. In addition, too much space in the pot is a welcome mat for plant diseases.

- **Try companion planting**

For many of us, nurseries, with all their beautiful displays of plants, can encourage impulse buying, which hardly produces the best results. You will need self-discipline and discretion to help you choose plants that will thrive and deliver excellent results in your location.

You will also need to select plants that will flourish in your particular light and climate conditions. Remember, taking a bunch of plants and growing them together will only lead to dissatisfaction! If you're planning on adding multiple species, then choose ones that share similar light, water, and soil requirements.

In addition, companion planting is a great way to enhance the visual appeal of your container garden. Not only that, but companion plants help neighbouring plants grow better by warding off certain insects.

Here are some ideas with which you can experiment:

- Lemonade garden – try planting Lemon Mint, Lemon Basil, and Lemon Balm in a planter. You'll need about a 20 inch (51 cm) or bigger pot.

- Pizza garden – you can plant Greek Oregano, Basil, and Tomatoes in a 22 inch (56 cm) or larger container.
- Mexican herb garden – here, you can add Greek Oregano, Parsley, Mint, and Thyme in a 16 inch (41 cm) or broader planter.
- You can even go for a classic combo garden that includes Basil and Tomato in an 18 inch (46 cm) pot. Basil doesn't only make Tomatoes taste better, but as a combination pair, they repel flies, mosquitoes, thrips, and more.

GROOM BI-WEEKLY

You may have noticed that many gardeners spend hours grooming their shrubs and trees in an attempt to control their shape and size. However, that's not the only reason for grooming.

Bi-weekly grooming (maintenance pruning) is a way to ensure you keep your container plants productive and healthy. By grooming your potted plants regularly, you ultimately inhibit plant problems. Plant diseases and pests gain access into a plant through broken branches, deadwood, and even through wounded branches (branches rubbing together).

You may think that this is only possible for grounded plants, but that isn't the case. Due to your container plants being so close together or having multiple plants in one pot, the reduced airflow may cause pests and fungi to spread more rapidly if not groomed regularly.

- **Grooming guidelines**

It's one thing to do maintenance pruning often; it's another to know how to do it properly. By considerately cutting back stems, limbs, and branches, you promote new growth that creates abundant fruit and flowers; it also thwarts the spread of disease and pests.

Anyone will tell you to prune your plants regularly. I know this doesn't offer much help. You need to know what to cut, where to cut, and when to cut. If you're new to pruning, this topic can seem overwhelming at first, especially if you're unsure where to start and which plants to consider. So here are a few tips below:

- What to cut: broken branches, wounded branches, sprawling/disheveled stems.
- Where to cut: never cut straight, always cut at an angle just beyond the buds situated immediately above a branch leaf.
- When to cut: it's time to prune when your branches/stems are dead or ailing. To check whether a limb is alive or dead, gently scratch the stem with a set of trimmers to see the color. If it's brown, it's lifeless and should be pruned. If it's green, it's alive.
- If the disease is attacking your plants: cut about 6 inches (15 cm) into the healthy branch. You want to get rid of the diseased part and stop it from spreading.

- **Watch out**

Checking for grooming needs is also a chance to observe any imperfections or abnormalities within your plants. To keep your plants free from disease and pest invasion, monitor your plants regularly and remove any abnormal-looking or diseased varieties as quickly as possible. In addition, be on the lookout for some common problems listed below.

- Powdery mildew – this fungus looks like someone dusted your foliage with powder. Prevent it by using neem oil or a weak solution of bicarb and water.
- Black spot – targets fruit plants and looks like black or brown specks on leaves and stems. Remove these stems and leaves. Neem oil can prevent this too.
- Botrytis blight – attacks veggies and other fruit and looks like gray mold. Prevent this by watering the plant roots and not the leaves or fruit themselves. Get rid of infected plants.
- Rust – looks like rust spots on stems and leaves. Do not overwater plants and avoid overhead watering as well.

Scan this QR code using your phone's camera to learn about the most common pests that may plague your plants and how to combat them.

CONSIDER DWARF VARIETIES

Dwarf varieties don't require a large growing area and are well-matched for containers, so having an urban garden or a little outdoor space doesn't have to restrict you. Because the fruits, veg, and plants are smaller in size, you cannot expect them to perform like full-sized varieties.

In saying that, dwarf varieties are easier to manage than full-sized plants and can enhance entrances, decks, and patios. In addition, you can make your porch feel more like a garden, and if you decide to plant dwarf fruit trees, you can enjoy the fruits as well. If you have a more spacious garden, then choosing to plant potted trees provides striking focal points that add stature and drama when placed on either side of doorways or entrances.

- **Selection process**

Planting trees in containers and grow bags has become popular, especially in gardens with little space. As long as you have a balcony, a porch, deck, or patio, you can grow trees in large containers. Beginner gardeners need to start small in their first year of gardening. Having too many plants and managing too many varieties will become a stressful chore and will not be an enjoyable hobby.

Whether you choose 'dwarf' or 'bush' varieties of vegetables or fruits, select them using the same criteria you would for picking any other plant. You need to choose types that will flourish in your climate and make sure you take moisture and light exposure into account.

SEED SAVING

Seed saving requires choosing suitable plants from which to gather seeds. The seeds will need to be harvested at the opportune time and have a proper storage place during winter. It's an excellent idea to gather seeds from your garden crops to plant the following year.

You can cut your gardening costs quite a bit when you decide to save seeds from previously purchased plants, whether it's fruit, veg, or flowers. If seed saving is something you're considering, you need to know how to care for them. Do some research if you're planning to keep and grow them.

- ## Types of seed to save

When selecting seeds to save, choose self-pollinating plants. Peppers, Beans, and Tomatoes are often a good selection for seed collection because they have self-pollinating flowers and require little to no special treatment before storing them. Plants that are cross-pollinators (separate male and female flowers), like vine crops, are more difficult to save because the seed strain is rarely pure.

While cross-pollination won't affect the current crop's quality, the seeds it produces are not like ones from the parent plant, which means flavor profiles and other characteristics may be inferior. Select parent plants that are strong and healthy. If they produce anything edible, make sure they're tasty too. Please never save seeds from off-type or weak, sickly plants, or you'll get a poor harvest in the following year if you manage to grow them.

- ## Seed storage

When selecting containers to store the seeds you've collected from your garden, opt for ones that will keep them dry. Since dryness is the key to proper seed storage, you'll want something that will not allow water or residue to invade the seed container. While you can use any material for this, I assure you that paper is best, and it's also inexpensive!

If you opt for paper storage (most advisable), choose coin envelopes, seed packets, improvise by getting bank envelopes, etc., and seal them with tape. If you decide to go with plastic, glass, or canisters, make sure they are properly dry inside and seal tightly. It's a good idea to mark your envelopes/containers with the date of seed collection, the name of the seed, and any other relevant information you may need later.

MULCHING

Adding mulch to your plants is more beneficial than you realize. In addition to providing moisture to your soil, it acts as an insulator to protect your plants, suppresses weeds, and adds color and texture to your container garden to make it attractive.

Organic mulches are particularly useful in encouraging the presence of earthworms which are great for keeping your soil aerated. These mulches also add traces of nutrients such as potassium, nitrogen, phosphorus, and other elements to your potting mix. Organic mulches make use of wood chips, shredded bark, pine needles, shredded leaves, and straw, and it's a great way to make use of recycled yard waste.

Inorganic mulch consists of gravel, stone, plastic, and other crushed products and tends to be a more effective barrier against weeds. Plastic and aluminized mulches will support your veggie plants by increasing their yield and better controlling pests. It's also a better alternative to pesticides and herbicides.

- **Let's keep our soil moist**

Are you finding that sticking to a watering schedule can be challenging? Most newbie gardeners do struggle with this in the beginning. If you don't have time to water plants that need it frequently, you should consider mulching. Mulching helps keep the soil moist and is especially effective if your plants are water-sensitive or out in the sun all day. Place 1 inch (2.5cm) of mulch on the surface of your potting mix in the container, but space it away from plant stems. Once you apply mulch, keep it there. Removing it may potentially injure plant roots. Also, avoid too much mulch as it will cause roots to grow shallowly, which is dangerous for a plant in dry weather.

- **Decoration**

Mulching makes plants look attractive as well, so in addition to using it for water retention, consider using it to make your plants look eye-catching. Newbie gardeners love to go all out and mulch around trees planted in containers as it looks attractive. However, mounding mulch against your tree can lead to bark rot, insect problems, and various diseases. To prevent infestation and disease, spread the mulch so that it extends from the tree base and mulch higher around the edges of the container. Woody or bark mulches look attractive around trees and flowers, while lighter materials like straw are better for your veggie containers.

PAINTED POTS

If you find the containers and grow bags you're using boring, why not consider painting them? My kids love getting involved in sprucing up old or boring containers – it's quite a tradition in my home.

You can change colors to look appealing, but be selective because some colors can be detrimental to your plant. For example, using darker color paints on your containers will absorb more heat than light-colored ones and may cause your potting soil to dry up as the weather heats up.

If your pot is in full sun, avoid using the color black as it will absorb the sun's rays in summer, and increased heat can cook the roots. However, dark-colored pots can be an asset in winter if you're leaving them outside, so always determine your plant's final location before painting and decide if you need to bring it indoors or take it outdoors as the seasons change. If you're living in a hot climate, I'd recommend light-colored containers to keep your plant's roots cool.

- **Painting as an activity**

Choosing non-toxic waterproof paint is essential. Not sure which color to use? Try white! It's eye-catching and goes with almost anything. Green can clash and distract you from the plant's foliage, so you might want to refrain from this as a single solid color. Allow your creative side to shine with the designs and color schemes you choose. At the same time, always decorate with your plant in mind.

If you have attractive, showy plants, opt for simple colors with fewer designs, as this will make your plant stand out. If you are designing a pot for a simple plant, you can get creative and make it an attractive focal point of your outdoor space. Applying paint with a foam brush will give your container a nice texture and help paint quickly. Use thinner brushes and different colors to add intricate designs and patterns.

- **Spruce up your space**

Choose paints to match your décor. Then, you can personalize the containers by adding your unique style. Consider adding decorations like ribbons around small containers to make them cute. You could also paint your plant's name on a stone and place it near your container as an attractive plant marker.

Finally, you can add creative DIY signboards to make your container plant space attractive, and you can even use them to add some humor to your garden. Signs like "Gardeners believe that what goes down must come up" or "We're mint to be" are sure to put a smile on your face when you pass by your container garden.

BEST TIME TO WATER

Pouring water over a plant doesn't necessarily mean your plant will be happy. The time of day you water plays an equally important role. Consider several variables: full sun vs cloudy conditions, the wind, temperature, humidity, container type, and the stage of your plant growth when considering ideal watering times and quantities.

Also, remember watering requirements for plants may vary considerably, so you'll need to remember each plant's watering needs carefully and group container plants with the same watering needs together. Keep in mind that plants with thinner leaves tend to want a lot more water than thicker-leaved plants.

- **Consider the sun**

The best time of the day to water your plant is when the sun won't evaporate the water. The last thing you want is water evaporating into the air, leaving your feeder roots still wanting more (what a waste).

Another thing to consider is your method of watering. If you're using a hosepipe, you can reach all the plants on your patio, for example. However, if your hosepipe has been lying out in the sun, the water may be hot, and this could stunt the development of your plants' roots.

Also, if the foliage gets wet, it could be susceptible to sunscald and disease. Let all the hot water run out first before bringing the hose to your containers. If you have small containers, a watering can is fine. But don't forget that watering many plants, especially the big fruit trees means carrying a heavy watering can and is not good for your back, especially if you need to water plants often.

- **Water at dawn or before sunset**

Savvy gardeners know that watering plants at dawn or right before sunset are the best times to water plants. These times are usually the best times for plants to soak up the water. Never water your plants when it's already dark. Dawn and before the evening are relatively convenient for you either way. If you're a morning person, water your plants at dawn, or if you're coming home from work in the late afternoon, that's a good time to water your plants too.

FERTILIZER MIXES

When you water your plants as frequently as you should, with water coming out the drainage holes, nutrients like nitrogen which is water-soluble, are easily lost. Unlike plants in the ground that can expand their roots to find food, containers restrict plants giving them no access to fresh dirt and nutrition. We can use fertilizers to combat this problem.

When you add fertilizer before planting, you provide a successful start to plant growth. However, it would be best if you exercised restraint. Too much fertilizer is equally bad, if not worse than no fertilizer, and your plant roots may suffer damage from the excess salt accumulation and become vegetative. Over-fertilizing can also cause plant leaves to turn yellow or brown as the natural salts in fertilizers suck the plant's moisture and cause burning.

- **Vitamins and nutrients**

Supplying nitrogen, phosphorus, and potassium can be done with controlled-release, slow-release, or liquid fertilizers. You can add a micronutrient solution to provide boron, copper, zinc, manganese, and iron elements. Plant leaves can also absorb nutrients through a foliar fertilizer. A nitrogen-rich mix will promote leaf growth and seedlings, while a phosphorus solution will encourage blooming. Slow-release fertilizers will keep your plants flowering all season. You should always check first what type of nutrients the plant requires. You don't want lush foliage at the expense of fruit or veg production.

- **Fertilizer types**

A solution of all-purpose fertilizer, 24 – 8 – 16 (24% nitrogen, 8% phosphorous, and 16% potassium), will help most of your container plants. Take heed of how you dilute the fertilizer. Check the recommended dosage on the packaging. If the package says one scoop a month, you can split it into two portions for bi-weekly feedings or four for weekly feedings.

- Controlled-release fertilizers:

These are more expensive synthetic fertilizers, but they provide nutrients for several months and avoid high salt levels. When you apply a controlled-release fertilizer, add it to the top of the pot, allowing the nutrients to travel down the container, which increases the chance of your plant absorbing the nutrients. If your plant is outdoors in a windy area, mix it in before potting.

- Slow-release fertilizers:

These come in both organic and synthetic forms. Organic fertilizers have a low water solubility, prolonged nutrient release rates over the years, and are less concentrated than synthetic fertilizers. Slow-release fertilizer is suitable for container plants, but you can supplement it with a liquid fertilizer if you have a fast-growing plant.

- Liquid:

These are quick-release fertilizers and are desirable to use after plants are growing. They are cheap and quickly replace nutrients. They can be tricky to use in containers with mixed species of plants, so be careful how you use them.

- Granular:

These types of fertilizers are not time-released. You can work them into the top layer of your pot. Be careful with them as they can burn plant roots if they come in contact.

- Foliar:

These are sprays that quickly supply nutrients. You increase absorption when you allow the spray to reach the underside of the leaves, where the stomata are. Be careful when using this spray on plants in mixed containers.

WATCH FOR DEFICIENCIES

When you groom and maintain your plants, you get up close and personal with them so you can see weaknesses and problems immediately. Watch how they respond to your care and maintenance regime. If they are not happy with any conditions, they won't hesitate to let you know. They'll communicate through their appearance and the way they flourish.

156 | INTRODUCTION TO CONTAINER GARDENING

- **Signs of deficiencies**

Signs of deficiencies don't only include wilting or holes within plants. Slow growth, lackluster, leggy plants, and yellow/brown leaves are all shortcomings that you need to treat. With the application of a few simple steps and weekly maintenance, you can help your container plants to spring back to life.

- Leggy plants:

Scrawny, chicken leg plants are not attractive. Cutting back your plant forces new growth, so don't hesitate to prune.

- Brown/yellow leaves:

Leaching (when you've overwatered and washed the nutrients out), inadequate moisture, and overfertilizing are usually the culprits. Pay attention to watering and adjust your fertilizing routine. You'll also know whether you've neglected your plants or given them too much sunlight. Mulch to retain moisture or leave pots of water nearby your container plants on hot days. Water will evaporate, increasing moisture levels.

- Lackluster:

When plants are looking lifeless and dull, check that you meet their light requirements. Leaching nutrients from the soil from watering also causes under-performance, so your fertilizing regime may need to be revisited.

- **Observe the fruit and soil**

The most common cause of wilting is too much or too little water. If your plant is drooping, check the soil. If the soil is dry, water slowly until the water drains out the drainage holes. If the potting mix feels damp, cut back on watering until the soil is dry to the touch. Minor deficiencies may be plant-specific, so check out each plant accordingly.

Now you're fully equipped with all the tricks of the container and grow bag gardening trade that I have learned over the past five years. Of course, you're probably dying to get started on your own garden now, but before you go, please page over to the last section for a few last words.

CONCLUSION

Now that you're well-equipped with the basic knowledge required for container and grow bag gardening, there's only one thing left to do: get started!

I discovered over the years that container and grow bag gardening is a fabulous hobby for those who wish to eat their very own fresh fruit, veggies, and herbs. It's also great for homemakers who want to brighten up and beautify a balcony or small outdoor space. For me, it's more than just a hobby, it's a lifestyle, and I find it fulfilling. Container and grow bag gardening gives me every bit of the rewarding enjoyment that a large garden would, except it costs a lot less, requires less time and effort, and offers double the productivity. You're far more in control of the growing process when your plants are in containers and grow bags – trust me on that one!

Of course, as is the case with any hobby and project, there is a lot to consider when pursuing container and grow bag gardening. And hopefully, this book has made it easier to navigate the process, right from selecting the right containers/grow bags to harvesting delicious crops for your dinner table. When you have a handy guide like this, the entire process is made simpler, after all, there's no guesswork involved.

In this container and grow bag gardening guide, you learned how to prepare for container gardening and how to select a suitable container. You also learned all about choosing the ideal herbs, fruit, veggies, and flowers for grow bags and containers and gained insight into the common gardening problems that newbies often encounter. In addition to this, you learned a few tips and tricks for keeping your container and grow bag garden beautiful and thriving. I think we can all agree that you've now got all the grow bag and container gardening bases covered and you're primed and ready to start.

If you've been grappling with the idea of starting your own garden for some time but have felt overwhelmed and under-equipped for the process, now is the time to put that thinking aside. The choices may seem intimidating, and the gardening process might seem time-consuming, but in reality, with the basics in mind, you can easily create a container and grow bag space that keeps giving back. The choices aren't all that diffi-cult to make when you have a foundation!

If you enjoyed reading this book and found it helpful for newbie gardeners, I warmly encourage you to share your opinion with others by leaving an honest review that can help others who might be experiencing similar gardening fears, hesitations, and challenges as you. Please click on the QR code below, that's applicable to you.

If you're based in USA: https://www.amazon.com/review/create-review?asin=B09BG8JS51

If you're based in the UK: https://www.amazon.co.uk/review/create-review?asin=B09BG8JS51

With that said, there's only one thing left for *me* to say: happy container and grow bag gardening!

RESOURCES

10 Common Container Gardening Beginner Mistakes - Better Gardener's Guide. (2021, January 21). Better Gardener's Guide. https://bettergardeners.com/common-container-gardening-mistakes/

A. (2019, December 9). *How To Grow Green Onions | Growing Green Onions In Containers Year Round.* Balcony Garden Web. https://balconygardenweb.com/how-to-grow-green-onions-growing-green-onions-in-containers/

All You Need to Know About Figs. (2020, July 16). Trifocus Fitness Academy. https://trifocusfitnessacademy.co.za/blog/all-you-need-to-know-about-figs/

ALLONSY, A. (n.d.). *How to Waterproof a Wood Planter Box.* Hunker. Retrieved 10 June 2021, from https://www.hunker.com/13425611/how-to-waterproof-a-wood-planter-box

Antosh, G. (2021, June 25). *New Guinea Impatiens: How To Plant, Care For And Grow.* Plant Care Today. https://plantcaretoday.com/new-guinea-impatiens-care.html

Atkins, T. (2017, April 28). *Everything you always wanted to know about tomatoes but were afraid to ask. . . - Moulin du Fontcourt Riverside*

Apartment and Chambres d'Hotes Charente. Moulin Du Fontcourt Riverside Apartment and Chambres d'Hotes Charente. https://moulindufontcourt.com/everything-you-always-wanted-to-know-about-tomatoes-but-were-afraid-to-ask/

Baessler, L. (2020, March 23). *Petunia Container Care: Growing Petunias In Pots*. Gardening Know How. https://www.gardeningknowhow.com/ornamental/flowers/petunia/petunia-container-care.htm

Baley, A. (2021, April 26). *Information About New Guinea Impatiens: Caring For New Guinea Impatiens Flowers*. Gardening Know How. https://www.gardeningknowhow.com/ornamental/flowers/impatiens/new-guinea-impatiens.htm

BBC Gardeners' World Magazine. (2020a, June 16). *How to grow peaches and nectarines*. https://www.gardenersworld.com/how-to/grow-plants/how-to-grow-peaches-and-nectarines/

BBC Gardeners' World Magazine. (2020b, June 16). *How to grow peaches and nectarines*. https://www.gardenersworld.com/how-to/grow-plants/how-to-grow-peaches-and-nectarines/

BBC Gardeners' World Magazine. (2020c, June 30). *The best planters and containers for strawberries*. https://www.gardenersworld.com/plants/the-best-containers-for-strawberries/

BBC Gardeners' World Magazine. (2021, July 8). *How to grow strawberries*. https://www.gardenersworld.com/how-to/grow-plants/how-to-grow-strawberries/

Bielenberg, S. (2021, May 13). *Growing Cucumbers in a Pot | Gardener's Supply*. Gardeners Supply Company. https://www.gardeners.com/how-to/growing-cucumbers-in-pots/8854.html

Caring For Broccoli. (n.d.). Yardener. Retrieved 16 July 2021, from https://gardening.yardener.com/Caring-For-Broccoli

Container Garden Temperature, Moderating Temperature in Container Gardens. (n.d.). Grow It Organically. Retrieved 11 June 2021, from https://www.grow-it-organically.com/container-garden-temperature.html

Demos, K. (2019, June 3). *Pruning Tips and Techniques Guide for Beginners.* FineGardening. https://www.finegardening.com/article/pruning-tips-and-techniques

DIG Digital Marketing. (n.d.). *Container Gardening 104: Compatibility.* Plants for All Seasons. Retrieved 1 July 2021, from https://plantsforallseasons.com/container-gardening-104-compatibility/#heading1

Dwarf Trees To Grow In Containers. (2019, February 14). The Tree Center. https://www.thetreecenter.com/dwarf-trees-grow-containers/

Dyer, M. (2020, April 20). *Potted Mint Plants – How To Grow Mint In Containers.* Gardening Know How. https://www.gardeningknowhow.com/edible/herbs/mint/potted-mint-plants.htm#:~:text=Fill%20a%20container%20with%20quality,mint%2C%20and%20again%20every%20spring

Dyer, M. (2021, April 26). *Potted Rosemary Herbs: Caring For Rosemary Grown In Containers.* Gardening Know How. https://www.gardeningknowhow.com/edible/herbs/rosemary/rosemary-grown-in-containers.htm

FastGrowingTrees.com. (n.d.). *Fig Trees: Everything You Ever Wanted to Know.* Retrieved 2 July 2021, from https://www.fast-growing-trees.com/pages/fig-trees-guide

Fischer, N. (2018, February 21). *The History of Lettuce.* Motherearthgardener.Com. https://www.motherearthgardener.com/plant-profiles/the-history-of-lettuce-zm0z18szphe/

Forney, J. (n.d.). *Growing Tomatoes in Pots.* Bonnie Plants. Retrieved 3 June 2021, from https://bonnieplants.com/gardening/grow-tomatoes-pots/

G. (2020, April 16). *Can you grow squash in pots?* Gardening Channel. https://www.gardeningchannel.com/grow-squash-in-pots/

Garden Design Magazine. (2021a, April 7). *Sweet Potato Vine – How to Plant, Grow, and Care for Ipomea batatas.* GardenDesign.-Com. https://www.gardendesign.com/vines/sweet-potato-vine.html#care

Garden Design Magazine. (2021b, April 7). *Sweet Potato Vine – How to Plant, Grow, and Care for Ipomea batatas.* GardenDesign.-Com. https://www.gardendesign.com/vines/sweet-potato-vine.html#pictures

Garden Design Magazine. (2021c, July 12). *Petunias – A Guide to Planting & Growing Petunia Flowers.* GardenDesign.Com. https://www.gardendesign.com/annuals/petunias.html#basics

Garden Gate Magazine. (2021, May 12). *Meet 12 of the Best Container Plants.* Garden Gate. https://www.gardengatemagazine.com/articles/containers/all/meet-8-of-the-best-container-plants/

Gibson, A. (2018, April 19). *6 Easy DIY Container Garden Projects.* The Micro Gardener. https://themicrogardener.com/6-easy-diy-container-garden-projects/

Gibson, A. (2021, June 15). *Choosing a Pot Plant Container - The Pros and Cons.* The Micro Gardener. https://themicrogardener.com/choosing-a-container-the-pros-and-cons-2/

Grant, A. (2018, October 25). *Are Ornamental Sweet Potatoes Edible – Should You Be Eating Ornamental Sweet Potatoes.* Gardening Know How. https://www.gardeningknowhow.

com/edible/vegetables/sweet-potato/eating-ornamental-sweet-potatoes.htm

Grant, A. (2021, June 2). *Can Peach Trees Grow In Pots: Tips On Growing Peaches In A Container.* Gardening Know How. https://www.gardeningknowhow.com/edible/fruits/peach/growing-peaches-in-containers.htm

Grant, B. (2021a, June 22). *Care Of Persian Shield Plant: Tips For Growing Persian Shield Indoors.* Gardening Know How. https://www.gardeningknowhow.com/houseplants/persian-shield/growing-persian-shield-indoors.htm

Grant, B. (2021b, June 28). *Growing Thyme Indoors: How To Grow Thyme Indoors.* Gardening Know How. https://www.gardeningknowhow.com/edible/herbs/thyme/growing-thyme-indoors.htm

GreekBoston.com. (2020, December 14). *Greek Oregano: Cooking and Medicinal Info.* Greek Boston. https://www.greekboston.com/herbs-spices/oregano/

Grow Veg. (2014, March 28). *Container Gardening - Top Tips for Success.* YouTube. https://www.youtube.com/watch?v=zn6IWlvMuJE

Growing Broccoli. (n.d.). Gardening Know How. Retrieved 1 July 2021, from https://www.gardeningknowhow.com/edible/vegetables/broccoli/growing-broccoli-in-pots.html

Growing Fig Trees in Containers. (n.d.). Stark Bro's. Retrieved 23 June 2021, from https://www.starkbros.com/growing-guide/article/figs-on-wheels

Growing Fruit Trees in Containers, Part 1. (n.d.). Stark Bro's. Retrieved 16 June 2021, from https://www.starkbros.com/growing-guide/article/fruit-trees-in-containers-pt1

Growing Geraniums. (n.d.). Miracle Gro. Retrieved 17 June 2021, from https://www.miraclegro.com/en-us/library/flowers-landscaping/growing-geraniums#:~:text=If%20you're%20-planting%20geraniums,root%20ball%20and%20surround-ing%20soil

Growing Parsley In Pots | How To Grow Parsley In Containers And Its Care. (2020, September 16). Balcony Garden Web. https://balconygardenweb.com/growing-parsley-in-containers

Growing Squash: How to Plant, Grow, Harvest, and Store. (n.d.). Eartheasy Guides & Articles. Retrieved 2 July 2021, from https://learn.eartheasy.com/guides/growing-squash-how-to-plant-grow-harvest-and-store/

Growing Thyme Indoors. (n.d.). Gardening Know How. Retrieved 6 June 2021, from https://www.gardeningknowhow.com/edible/herbs/thyme/growing-thyme-indoors

Growing Vegetables in Containers. (2021, June 1). University of Maryland Extension. https://extension.umd.edu/resource/growing-vegetables-containers

Hanna, A. (2000, July). *Inorganic Mulch.* High Plains Gardening. http://www.highplainsgardening.com/mulch/inorganic-mulch

Harvard Health. (2012, June 30). *Backyard gardening: grow your own food, improve your health.* https://www.health.harvard.edu/blog/backyard-gardening-grow-your-own-food-improve-your-health-201206294984

Hassani, N. (2021, July 13). *The Difference Between Potting Soil and Potting Mix.* The Spruce. https://www.thespruce.com/difference-between-potting-soil-potting-mix-847812

Havergill, S. (2020, October 20). *'An apple a day keeps the doctor away', but what does it really mean?* Healthy Performance. https://

www.healthyperformance.co.uk/an-apple-a-day-keeps-the-doctor-away-but-what-does-it-really-mean/

Henderson, J. (2021, June 21). *Everything You Need to Know About Growing Oregano.* Kitchn. https://www.thekitchn.com/everything-you-need-to-know-about-growing-oregano-220612

How To Grow Apple In Pots: A Step By Step Guide. (2021, May 27). Gardener Know How. https://gardenerknowhow.com/how-to-grow-apple-in-pots-a-step-by-step-guide

How to Grow Spinach in Pots | Growing Spinach in Containers & Care. (2019, December 6). Balcony Garden Web. https://balconygardenweb.com/how-to-grow-spinach-in-pots-growing-spinach-in-containers-care/

How To Water Container Gardens. (n.d.). HGTV. Retrieved 5 June 2021, from https://hgtv.co.uk/outdoors/gardens/garden-styles-and-types/how-to-water-container-gardens

Iannotti, M. (2021a, April 26). *How Do You Pinch, Deadhead, and Cut Back in Your Perennial Garden?* The Spruce. https://www.thespruce.com/pinching-deadheading-cutting-back-1402475

Iannotti, M. (2021b, April 26). *How Do You Pinch, Deadhead, and Cut Back in Your Perennial Garden?* The Spruce. https://www.thespruce.com/pinching-deadheading-cutting-back-1402475

Iannotti, M. (2021c, May 27). *How to Grow the Iridescent Leaves of Persian Shield.* The Spruce. https://www.thespruce.com/persian-shield-strobilanthes-dyerianus-1402914

Impatiens hawkeri (New Guinea Hybrids, New Guinea Impatiens) | North Carolina Extension Gardener Plant Toolbox. (n.d.). North Carolina Extension Gardener Plant Box. Retrieved 11 July 2021, from https://plants.ces.ncsu.edu/plants/impatiens-hawkeri/

Instructables. (2017, November 5). *How to Make a Self Watering Container*. https://www.instructables.com/How-to-make-a-self-watering-container/

Interesting facts about cherries | Just Fun Facts. (2020, August 23). Just Fun Facts. http://justfunfacts.com/interesting-facts-about-cherry/

Jabbour, N. (2021a, January 29). *Growing great basil*. Savvy Gardening. https://savvygardening.com/growing-great-basil/

Jabbour, N. (2021b, May 28). *Growing green beans: learn how to plant, grow, and harvest a bumper crop of green beans*. Savvy Gardening. https://savvygardening.com/growing-green-beans/

Jabbour, N. (2021c, May 28). *The 7 best herbs for container gardening*. Savvy Gardening. https://savvygardening.com/best-herbs-for-container-gardening/

Kring, L. (2021a, April 20). *Keep Your Containers Looking Great With These 6 Simple Tricks*. Gardener's Path. https://gardenerspath.com/how-to/containers/tips-for-beautiful-garden-containers/

Kring, L. (2021b, April 20). *Keep Your Containers Looking Great With These 6 Simple Tricks*. Gardener's Path. https://gardenerspath.com/how-to/containers/tips-for-beautiful-garden-containers/

L. Grant, B. (2021a, June 27). *How To Grow Lettuce In A Container*. Gardening Know How. https://www.gardeningknowhow.com/edible/vegetables/lettuce/growing-lettuce-containers.html

L. Grant, B. (2021b, June 29). *How To Container Grow Eggplant Plants*. Gardening Know How. https://www.gardeningknowhow.com/edible/vegetables/eggplant/container-eggplant-plants.htm

Leech, M. J. S. (2018, October 9). *10 Proven Health Benefits of Blueberries*. Healthline. https://www.healthline.com/nutrition/10-proven-benefits-of-blueberries

Link, M. R. S. (2017, October 27). *6 Science-Based Health Benefits of Oregano*. Healthline. https://www.healthline.com/nutrition/6-oregano-benefits

McLean, E. (2021, April 22). *Are Concrete Planters Safe For Plants?* Artsy Pretty Plants. https://artsyprettyplants.com/concrete-planters-safe-plants/

Michaeld, K. (2020, July 17). *Learn 5 Tips for How to Grow Beautiful Basil in Pots*. The Spruce. https://www.thespruce.com/growing-basil-in-containers-848215

Michaels, K. (2020, September 14). *Keep Your Yard Fresh With a Mint Container Garden*. The Spruce. https://www.thespruce.com/growing-a-mint-container-garden-4125233

Michaels, K. (2021a, January 21). *10 Container Garden Tips for Beginners*. The Spruce. https://www.thespruce.com/ten-container-garden-tips-for-beginners-847854

Michaels, K. (2021b, February 19). *6 Basic Steps for Growing a Container Garden*. The Spruce. https://www.thespruce.com/container-garden-the-essentials-847853

Michaels, K. (2021c, April 15). *10 Common Container Gardening Mistakes and How to Avoid Them*. The Spruce. https://www.thespruce.com/common-container-gardening-mistakes-847796

Michaels, K. (2021d, April 16). *Here Are 5 Tips to Start a Container Garden*. The Spruce. https://www.thespruce.com/tips-for-planting-a-container-garden-847799#:%7E:text=Drainage%20Is%20Critical&text=1%20In%20a%20garden%20bed,for%20excess%20water%20to%20drain

Morgan, J. R. (2012, June 14). *Everything You Ever Wanted to Know About Peppers!* Bob's Market and Greenhouses. https://www.bobsmarket.com/blog/bsmarketblog.com/2012/06/everything-you-ever-wanted-to-know.html

Mulching Tips from the Pros. (n.d.). Love Your Landscape. Retrieved 18 June 2021, from https://www.loveyourlandscape.org/expert-advice/shrubs-and-flowers/basic-care/mulching-tips-from-the-pros/#:%7E:text=Use%20woody%20or%20bark%20mulches,replanting%20may%20be%20common%20place

Murphy, S. (2020, May 12). *How To Care For Calibrachoa (Million Bells) Hanging Baskets.* Wallish Greenhouses. https://wallishgreenhouses.ca/Blog-Post/How-To-Care-For-Calibrachoa-Million-Bells-Hanging-Baskets

NC State Extension Publications. (n.d.). *18. Plants Grown in Containers.* Retrieved 4 July 2021, from https://content.ces.ncsu.edu/extension-gardener-handbook/18-plants-grown-in-containers

Nolte, K. (n.d.). *Green Beans.* College of Agriculture and Life Sciences. Retrieved 2 June 2021, from https://cals.arizona.edu/fps/sites/cals.arizona.edu.fps/files/cotw/Green_Beans.pdf

Nordqvist, J. (2017, December 13). *Everything you need to know about rosemary.* Medical News Today. https://www.medicalnewstoday.com/articles/266370#_noHeaderPrefixedContent

Parsley. (2020, March 23). The Epicentre. https://theepicentre.com/spice/parsley/

Patterson, S. (2016, October 7). *How to Grow a Dwarf Plum in a Container.* Home Guides | SF Gate. https://homeguides.sfgate.com/grow-dwarf-plum-container-39823.html

Perry, L. (n.d.). *Calibrachoa*. University of Vermont Department of Plant and Soil Science. Retrieved 21 June 2021, from https://pss.uvm.edu/ppp/articles/calibrachoa.html

PREPAREDNESSMAMA, P. M. (2021, April 29). *5 Tips to Grow Blueberries in Pots*. PreparednessMama. https://preparednessmama.com/grow-blueberries-in-pots

Raspberries. (n.d.). In Depth Info. Retrieved 7 June 2021, from http://www.indepthinfo.com/raspberries/history.html

Raspberries In Pots. (n.d.). Gardening Know How. Retrieved 5 June 2021, from https://www.gardeningknowhow.com/edible/fruits/raspberry/raspberries-in-pots.html

Reddy, J. (2020a, May 13). *Growing Turnips in Containers, Turnips Plant Care*. Gardening Tips. https://gardeningtips.in/growing-turnips-in-containers-turnips-plant-care

Reddy, J. (2020b, September 16). *Growing Cherry Trees In Pots, Containers, Backyard*. Gardening Tips. https://gardeningtips.in/growing-cherry-trees-in-pots-containers-backyard#:%7E:text=Container%20grown%20Cherry%20trees%20require,or%20drill%20some%20in%20yourself

Rogers, C. (2020, February 13). *10 Facts About Geraniums That Gardeners Should Know*. Southern Living. https://www.southernliving.com/garden/flowers/geranium-flower

Rose, S. (2020, March 23). *The Secrets to Successful Container Gardening*. Garden Therapy. https://gardentherapy.ca/successful-container-gardens/

Rosemary. (2009). The Herb Society Of America. https://www.herbsociety.org/file_download/inline/824d2982-0b7c-40d9-b3d9-9e5d823d295c#:~:text=History%20and%20Origin,the%20early%20Greeks%20and%20Romans

Saving vegetable seeds. (n.d.). UMN Extension. Retrieved 5 July 2021, from https://extension.umn.edu/planting-and-growing-guides/saving-vegetable-seeds

Shinn, M. (2019, December 9). *The Best Containers in Which to Save Garden Seeds*. Horticulture. https://www.hortmag.com/headline/the-best-containers-in-which-to-save-garden-seeds

Smart Garden Guide. (2019a, December 9). *How To Identify, Fix And Prevent Root Rot*. https://smartgardenguide.com/root-rot/

Smart Garden Guide. (2019b, December 9). *How To Identify, Fix And Prevent Root Rot*. https://smartgardenguide.com/root-rot/

Spengler, T. (2020, November 30). *Raspberry Container Care: How To Plant Raspberries In Pots*. Gardening Know How. https://www.gardeningknowhow.com/edible/fruits/raspberry/raspberries-in-pots.htm

Susan, M. (n.d.). *10 Container Gardening Mistakes to Avoid*. Proven Winners. Retrieved 27 May 2021, from https://www.provenwinners.com/learn/top-ten-lists/10-container-gardening-mistakes-avoid

Texas A&M AgriLife Extension Service. (2018, March 29). *Container Gardening – vegetables that grow in containers*. https://agrilifeextension.tamu.edu/solutions/container-gardening/

The Editors of Encyclopaedia Britannica. (n.d.). *basil | Definition, Uses, & Facts*. Encyclopedia Britannica. Retrieved 22 June 2021, from https://www.britannica.com/plant/basil

The Old Farmer's Almanac. (2020, October 29). *Peaches*. Old Farmer's Almanac. https://www.almanac.com/plant/peaches

Tilley, N. (2021a, April 7). *Growing Calibrachoa Million Bells: Growing Information And Calibrachoa Care*. Gardening Know

How. https://www.gardeningknowhow.com/ornamental/ flowers/million-bells/calibrachoa-million-bells.htm

Tilley, N. (2021b, June 14). *Growing Geraniums: Tips For The Care Of Geraniums*. Gardening Know How. https://www. gardeningknowhow.com/ornamental/flowers/geranium/ geranium-care.htm

User, S. (n.d.). *Grow the Best - Petunia Time*. Plant Care | Eckards Garden Pavilion. Retrieved 5 July 2021, from https:// eckards.co.za/plant-care/petunia-time

Vanheems, B. (2014, January 14). *How to Grow Strawberries Successfully in Containers*. GrowVeg. https://www.growveg.co.za/ guides/how-to-grow-strawberries-successfully-in-containers/

Vinje, E. (2018a, May 21). *Container Gardening Tips*. Planet Natural. https://www.planetnatural.com/container-gardening-tips/

Vinje, E. (2018b, May 21). *Fertilizing Potted Plants*. Planet Natural. https://www.planetnatural.com/fertilizing-potted-plants/#:%7E:text=A%20fertilizer%20high%20in% 20nitrogen,meal%20and%20liquid%20fish%20emulsion

What Are the Environmental Benefits of Growing Your Own Food? (2017, April 27). Triangle Pest Control. https://www. trianglepest.com/blog/what-are-environmental-benefits-growing-your-own-food

What Everyone Should Know About Plums. (n.d.). Solesoups. Retrieved 12 June 2021, from https://solesoups.com/2019/ 09/12/this-is-what-everyone-should-know-about-plums-lunch/

Wikipedia contributors. (2021, July 12). *Impatiens*. Wikipedia. https://en.wikipedia.org/wiki/Impatiens

Wiley, D. (2020, June 2). *How to Grow Delicious Berries in Containers*. Better Homes & Gardens. https://www.bhg.com/gardening/container/plans-ideas/berries-in-containers/

Zach, Z. (2021, July 9). *How to Grow Radishes in Containers*. Dengarden. https://dengarden.com/gardening/Grow-Radishes-in-Containers

Zamarripa, M. (2019a, April 5). *8 Impressive Health Benefits and Uses of Parsley*. Healthline. https://www.healthline.com/nutrition/parsley-benefits#TOC_TITLE_HDR_6

Zamarripa, M. (2019b, April 5). *8 Impressive Health Benefits and Uses of Parsley*. Healthline. https://www.healthline.com/nutrition/parsley-benefits#TOC_TITLE_HDR_6

Zimmerman, R. (2014, April 25). *Containing Mint*. FineGardening. https://www.finegardening.com/article/containing-mint

CPSIA information can be obtained
at www.ICGtesting.com
Printed in the USA
BVHW051046270122
627355BV00004B/262